SS UNIFORMS, INSIGNIA & ACCOUTREMENTS

SS UNIFORMS, INSIGNIA & ACCOUTREMENTS

A Study in Photographs

Compiled by A. Hayes

Schiffer Military History
Atglen, PA

Acknowledgements

A work of this size would not be possible without help from many people. My good friend Jon A. Maguire, author of four books on USAAF memorabilia, agreed to assist me with organization, text, and photography on this project. His experience and expertise were extremely valuable.

My heartfelt thanks go to Bob Biondi, Peter Schiffer, Mike Wipf, Jess Lutkins, Dick Heuvelen, Gordon Henger, Dave Delich, William P. Moran, Joe Stairrett, Mike Conner, Mike Whitson, Mike Davidson, L. Bloomer, C. Craig, and Rhonda Maguire.

Also a note of special thanks to my wife Susan for her continued support.

Book Design by Robert Biondi.

Copyright © 1996 by A. Hayes.
Library of Congress Catalog Number: 95-72358.

Printed in China.
ISBN: 0-7643-0046-6

We are interested in hearing from authors with book ideas on related topics.

Published by Schiffer Publishing Ltd.
77 Lower Valley Road
Atglen, PA 19310
Please write for a free catalog.
This book may be purchased from the publisher.
Please include $2.95 postage.
Try your bookstore first.

Contents

Auch Du

Introduction

The history of the SS has been examined and recorded in numerous volumes. Many fine authors have written of their fanatical dedication, tenacity, and bravery in battle, and of their horrendous atrocities. The uniforms they wore in ceremony and on the battlefield were beautiful, to the point of being garish, and symbolic of the role they played. The "Death's Head" insignia, which was so prevalent, was indeed appropriate. The subject of SS uniforms and insignia has also been well recorded, yet, there remains a desire among collectors and historians for more information. The fact that one organization, which existed for such a relatively short period, could have so much regalia associated with it is amazing! It also may explain why the material is highly collectible.

Perhaps more than any other area in the field of Militaria, SS collectors are faced with a marketplace rampant with fakes and frauds. When I began collecting SS material I was taken advantage of on several occasions. My education was very expensive! Although this subject has indeed been covered from a technical and historical perspective, few people ever have the opportunity to examine authentic material to any great extent. The old adage holds true that "a picture is worth a thousand words" – this is the reason for assembling this book. I sincerely hope it will help other collectors avoid unfortunate and costly mistakes. It is by no means a complete work on the subject, however it is a thorough examination of genuine SS material. Commentary has purposely been held to a minimum. It is my belief that every item in this book is of the period, but I am sure there are readers who may disagree with me on some of the pieces herein. Every effort has been made to ensure authenticity.

In no way is this book intended to glorify the actions or memories of the SS. It is simply a photographic record of some of the uniforms, insignia, and accoutrements they used.

CHAPTER 1
UNIFORMS & INSIGNIA

The black service uniform of an SS-Obersturmführer assigned to the 3rd SS Totenkopf-Standarte "Thuringen."

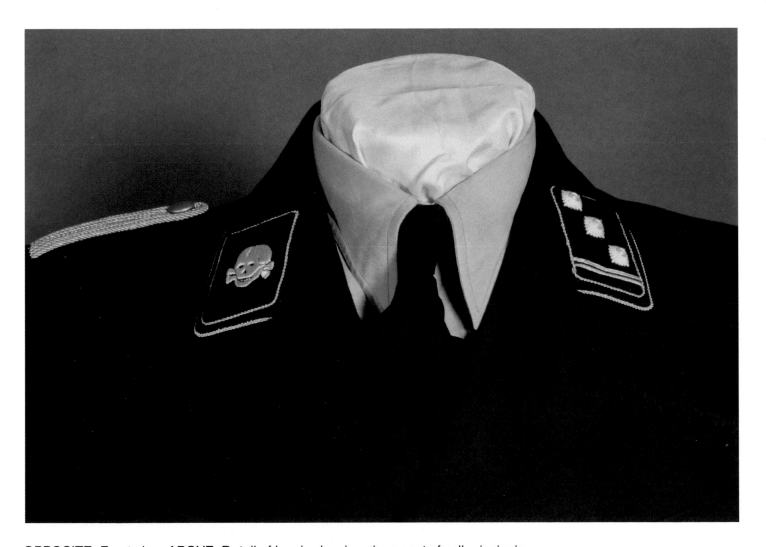

OPPOSITE: Front view. ABOVE: Detail of lapels showing placement of collar insignia.

Detail of "Totenkopf" collar tab.

Detail of Obersturmführer collar insignia.

Underside of lapel. Note the prongs from the collar tab rank pips go completely through the lapel.

Underside of lapel with silver piping hand-stitched in place.

Tailor's label in back of collar.

Tailor's label inside coat pocket with owner's name and 1938 date.

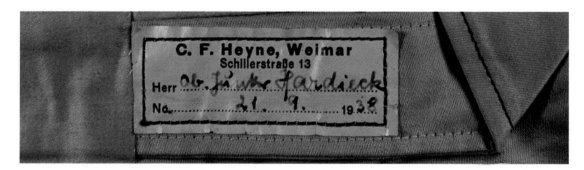

This label is inside the breeches.

Tailor's label in collar of shirt.

"D" ring inside coat for attaching the dagger hanger.

Reverse of uniform coat button – note "RZM" marking.

Detail of shoulder cord.

Detail of "Thuringen" sleeveband.

Detail of SS-Kampfbinde (Brassard).

Detail of Alter-Kampfer chevron. (Honor Chevron for old campaigners).

The black service uniform of an SS-Oberscharführer assigned to the SS-Standarte "Germania."

OPPOSITE: Front view.

Detail of lapel and chest area.

Collar insignia SS-Standarte "Germania."

Sleeveband detail.

Collar insignia SS-Oberscharführer.

Left sleeve with brassard and "Germania" sleeveband.

Markings on leather belt.

The black service uniform coat of an SS-Sturmbannführer with a specialty in administrative services – "Fulda-Werra."

LEFT: Front and back. RIGHT: This SS-Hauptsturmführer of SS-Standarte "Germania" wears the black service uniform.

Detail of Fulda-Werra sleeveband.

Detail of sleeve diamond, which indicated a specialty in administrative services.

Tag affixed to the reverse of sleeve brassard.

Alter-Kampfer chevron.

Detail of sleeve brassard.

Shoulder cord detail.

Black service uniform coat worn by an SS-Oberführer of SS Sub-District XXX.

Front view.

Collar insignia.

SS Brassard on left sleeve.

SS Sub-District XXX sleeveband detail.

Alter-Kampfer chevron on right shoulder.

Shoulder cord detail.

RZM tag on underside of shoulder cord.

Well marked button from shoulder. The "A" is the mark of Assman.

The SS Adjutant Aiguillette.

Detail of the aiguillette hanging tips. Note SS Runes.

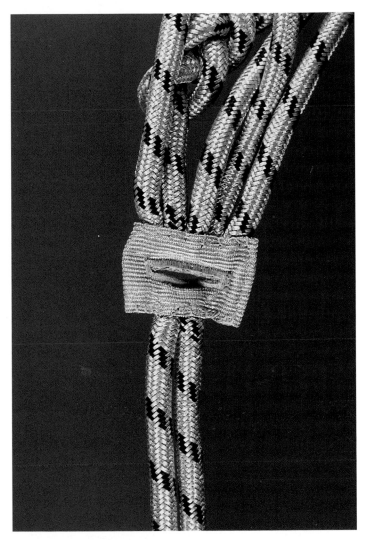

Detail of button attachment point where the aiguillette was affixed to the shoulder under the shoulder cord.

Detail of loop, which went around the top button of the uniform coat.

OPPOSITE: Front view. ABOVE: Lapel and pocket detail of right chest area.

Detail of right collar insignia.

Left collar insignia – rank of SS-Untersturmführer.

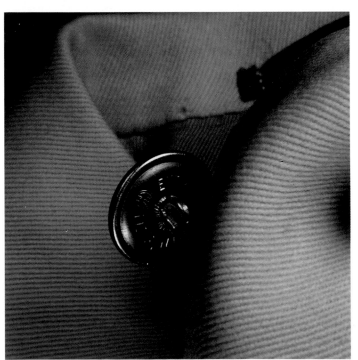

Markings on reverse of buttons.

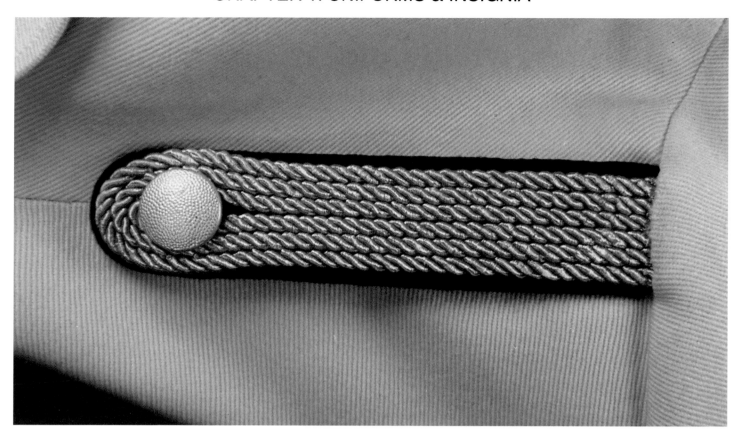

Shoulder cord.

Tailor's label sewn in back of collar.

Field gray uniform coat worn by a Waffen SS-Hauptsturmführer of the regiment "Nordland."

OPPOSITE: Front view. The red piping on the Army style shoulder boards (original to this uniform) indicate this man was an artillery officer. ABOVE: Left side view with "Nordland" sleeveband and sleeve eagle visible.

Detail of "Nordland" sleeveband.

Tailor's label in collar.

Tailor's label inside pocket with owner's name and date of 4/8/43.

Dagger hanger inside coat.

Three of these officers are wearing this style of uniform.

Field gray uniform coat worn by an SS-Obersturmführer of the "SS-Standarte Kurt Eggers", which was a regiment of SS-War Correspondents. SS War Correspondents wore standard SS uniforms. Early on they wore white piping and later, lemon-yellow, as seen in this example.

Front view. *(Heuvelen)*

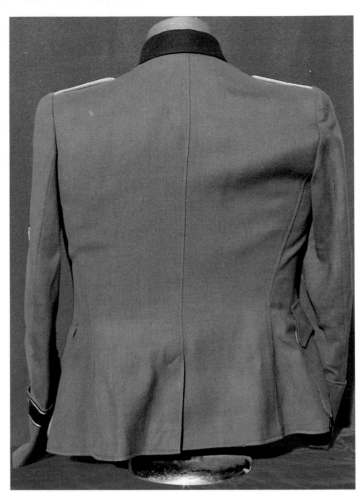

Left side with sleeve eagle and sleeveband visible. *(Heuvelen)*   Back of "Kurt Eggers" coat. *(Heuvelen)*

Collar insignia detail. *(Heuvelen)*

Detail of "Kurt Eggers" sleeveband. *(Heuvelen)*`

Sleeve eagle detail. *(Heuvelen)*

Shoulder board with lemon-yellow piping (Waffenfarbe) for War Correspondents. *(Heuvelen)*

The dress uniform of a full member of the SS serving in the German Police.

Front view.

Rear view.

Detail of cartouche and cross strap.

Police insignia on left sleeve.

Detail of left chest area. SS runes under the chest pocket indicates the man was a full member of the SS.

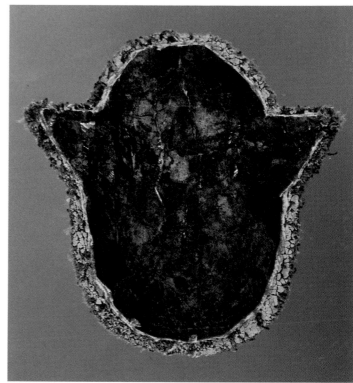

Detail of a police sleeve insignia – front and back.

Round patch variation of the SS-Runes (front and back) for wear under the left chest pocket, indicating full membership in the SS.

Detail of dress belt and buckle. Note SS runes woven into the belt itself.

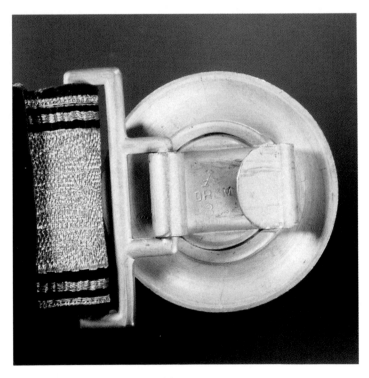

Reverse of dress belt buckle.

RIGHT: Police officers in Parade Dress.

The Police officer's dress shako. Note padding under eagle plate, which should be present on officer's shako.

The Field Police Gorget – front and back.

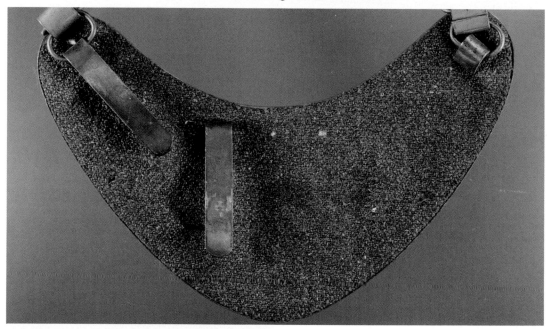

LEFT: The "A" mark of Assman is visible on this gorget.

OPPOSITE: A post card of the period with an SS man at left and an SD man at right.

Overcoat of an SS-Oberführer of SS Sub-District XXX.

Overcoat of an SS-Untersturmführer of the SD.

ABOVE: Overall front view. BELOW: Detail of lapel.

ABOVE and BELOW: Front view and left sleeve views.

An unissued overcoat for non-commissioned officers.

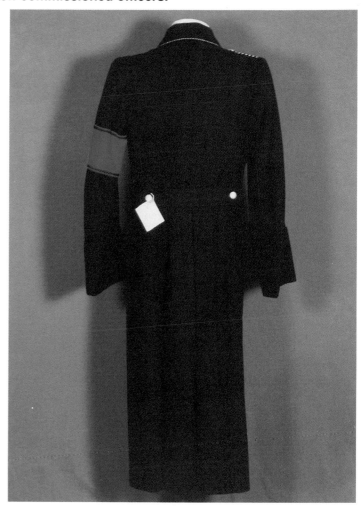

Front and back.

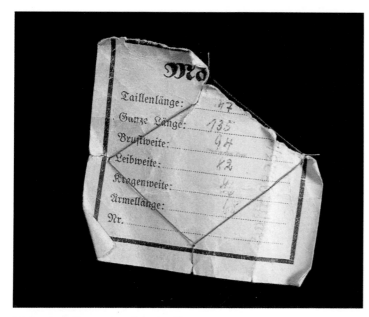

Maker's information label still attached to left sleeve.

SS label tied to button on the back side.

Black leather officer's overcoat.

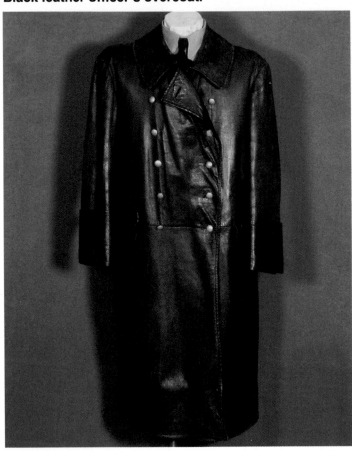

ABOVE: Front view. BELOW: Shoulder detail – note loop for attaching shoulder boards.

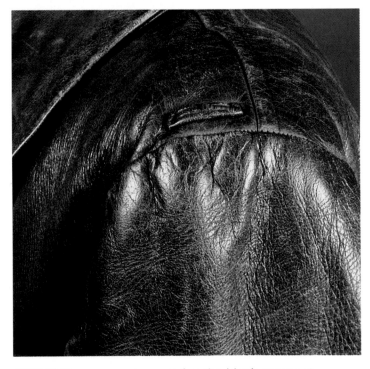

RIGHT: These men are wearing the black overcoat.

Overcoat of an SS-Sturmbannführer of SS-District (SS-Oberabschnitte) "Fulda-Werra."

Front view.

This officer is wearing a similar styled overcoat to the example at left.

Detail of "Fulda-Werra" sleeveband.

Detail of SS-Sturmbannführer collar insignia.

Detail of shoulder cord.

Sleeve eagle sewn to left arm.

Tailor's label in collar.

Tailor's label in pocket with owner's name.

CHAPTER 1: UNIFORMS & INSIGNIA

Green leather Waffen-SS officer's overcoat.

LEFT and ABOVE: Front and back views.

BELOW: Detail of shoulder with button and strap for attaching shoulder boards.

These officers are wearing variations of the overcoat.

Several overcoats are visible in this photograph taken early in the war.

Waist length dress cape for an SS officer. It was first thought this was a full length cape which had been cut down, but it appears this garment was custom made at this length.

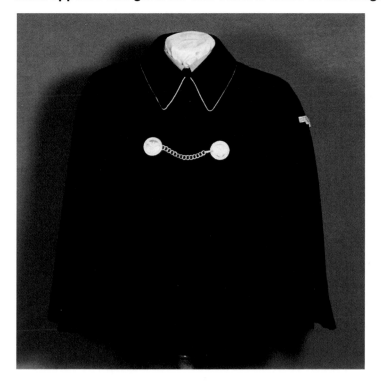

Front view.

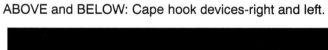

ABOVE and BELOW: Cape hook devices-right and left.

This photo shows how the cape hook devices are attached from the back side.

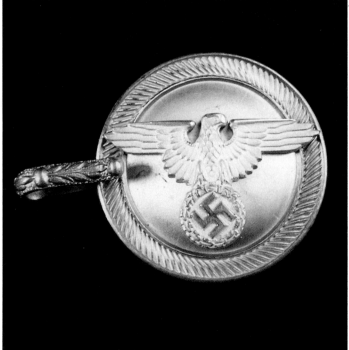

Tailor's label in collar.

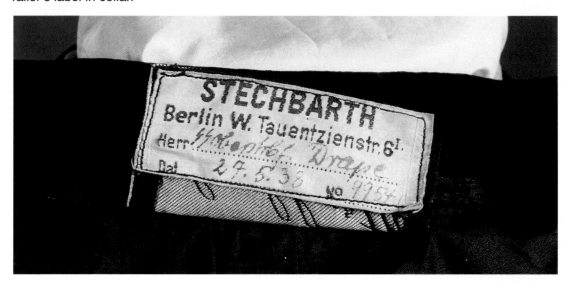

This name tag is sewn to the back of the tailor's label.

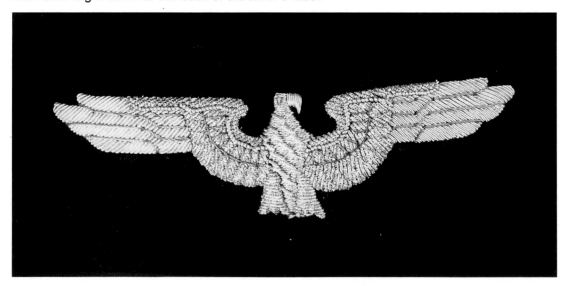

Detail of de-Nazified (Swastika has been removed) sleeve eagle.

The SS Neck Tie.

The official tie worn by men of the SS features this woven gray band at both ends.

SS Sleevebands or "Cuff Titles."

All ranks of the SS wore sleevebands which identified the unit in which they served. Sleevebands are a subject in themselves, as there are numerous types, and many variations of each type. I have provided several original period pieces for your examination.

Sleeveband for Leibstandarte SS "Adolf Hitler" (second version).

Detail of "Adolf."

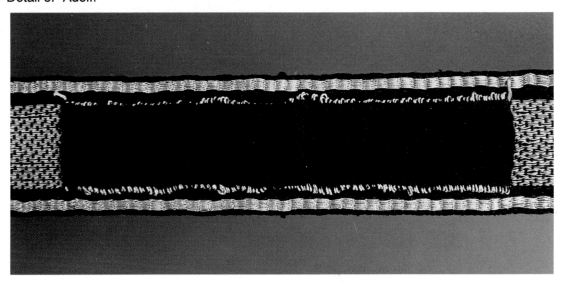

Reverse.

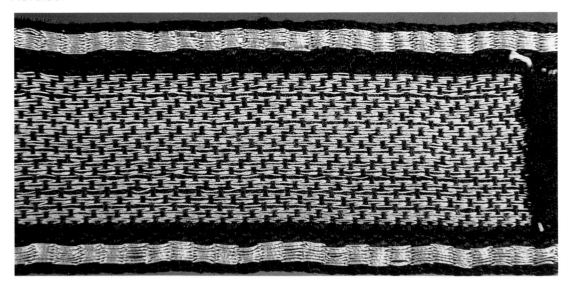

Detail of back.

Another variation of Leibstandarte "Adolf Hitler."

Detail of "Adolf" in this variation.

RZM tag affixed.

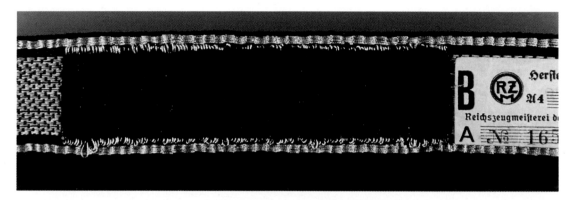

Hand embroidered sleeveband from SS-Standarte "Deutschland" – front and back. Note paper RZM tag.

Sleeveband of an enlisted man of the 1st SS Foot Regiment (SS-Foot Standarte 1 Munchen) "Julius Schreck" – front and back.

Hand embroidered sleeveband of an officer assigned to the 3rd SS-Totenkopf-Standarte "Thuringen" front and back.

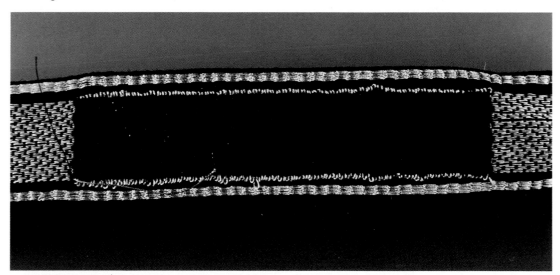

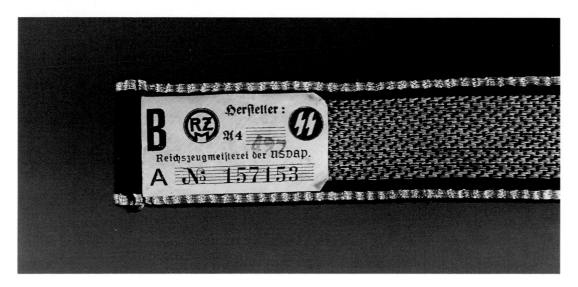

RZM tag affixed to reverse.

Hand embroidered sleeveband for 2. SS-Panzer-Division "Das Reich" front and back.

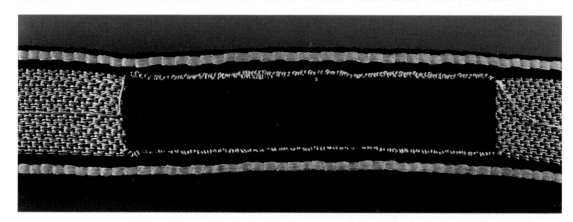

Front and back of "RZM Pattern" sleeveband for SS- Panzer-Grenadier-Regiment "Der Führer" in Latin script.

Officer's gothic script machine embroidered sleeveband for SS-Standarte "Der Führer" front and back.

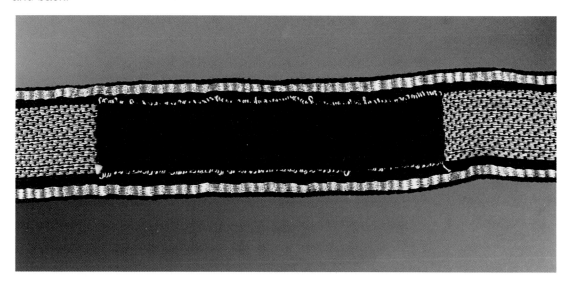

RZM tag.

SS-Totenkopf-Rekruten-Standarte "Oberbayern" machine embroidered sleeveband, front and back.

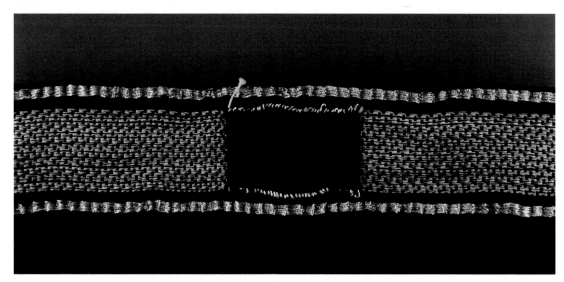

RZM tag on reverse.

A second variation of the SS-Totenkopf-Rekruten-Standarte "Oberbayern" hand embroidered sleeveband, front and back.

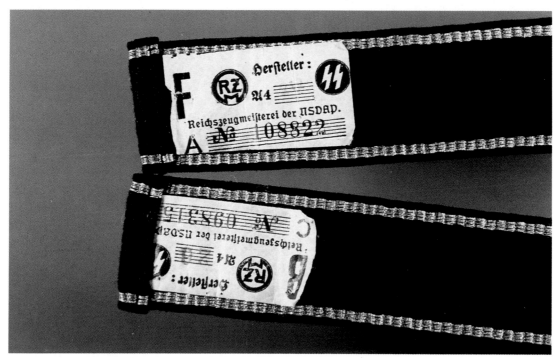

RZM tags on both ends.

Hand embroidered sleeveband for a medical company under command of SS Sub-District XXXXIII, front and back.

Sleeveband for an officer on staff of the 12th SS-Foot Standarte Hannover, front and back.

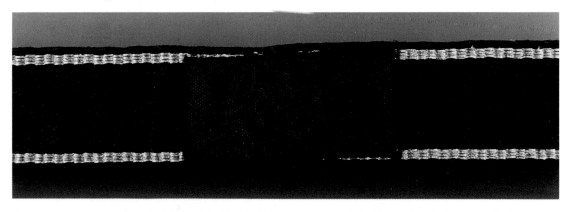

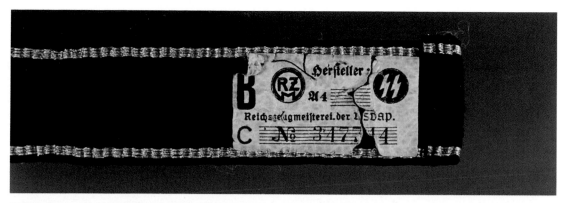

RZM tag for 12th SS-Foot Standarte Hannover sleeveband.

Sleeveband – 1st pattern "SS-Schule Tolz" (Officer Candidate School).

Collar Insignia

As was the case for sleevebands, collar insignia, commonly referred to as "tabs" or "patches", are a massive study. This section simply provides the reader with some period examples.

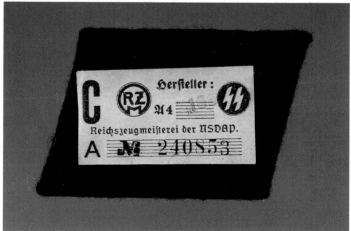

Front and back – NCO SS-Runes for wear on the right collar.

A second variation of the SS-Runes, NCO collar tab.

 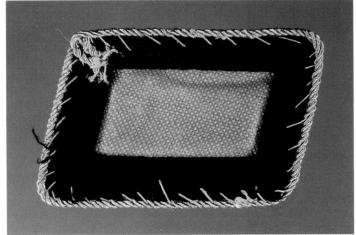

Officers of the Sicherheitsdienst (SD) wore a blank collar patch on the right collar (front and back).

Left collar patch of an SS-Sturmbannführer.

Front and back – collar patch of an SS-Obergruppenführer.

Front and back – a second example of an SS-Obergruppenführer's collar patch.

 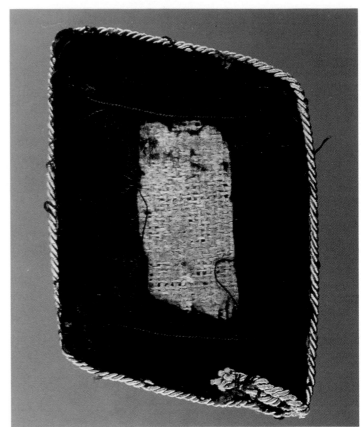

Front and back – left collar patch of an SS-Standartenführer.

 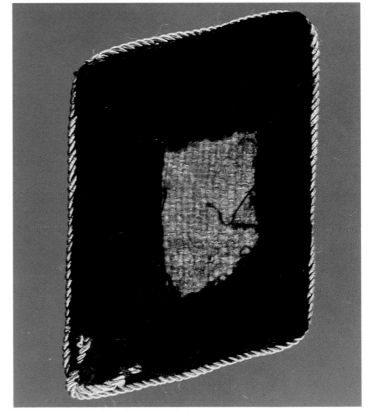

Front and back – right collar patch of an SS-Standartenführer.

CHAPTER 1: UNIFORMS & INSIGNIA

The National Emblem for the sleeve – "SS Sleeve Eagles."

Hand-embroidered first pattern SS officer's sleeve eagle.

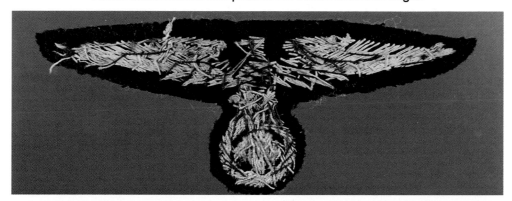

Front and back, of the standard SS officer's sleeve eagle, hand-embroidered of aluminum thread. Note how the Swastikas fill the circle.

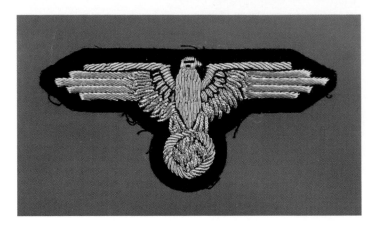

Another example of the standard SS officer's sleeve eagle, hand-embroidered of aluminum thread.

This beautifully detailed, high quality eagle was for wear on the dress cape.

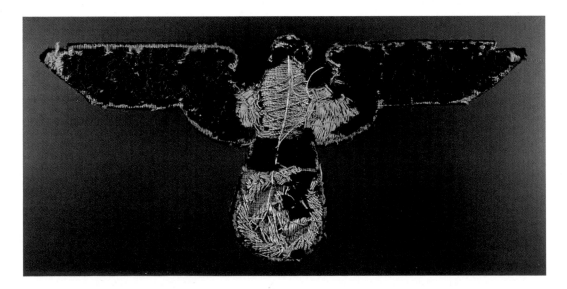

Machine embroidered SS sleeve eagle in tan for wear on camouflage and tropical uniforms.

Machine woven sleeve eagle for enlisted men.

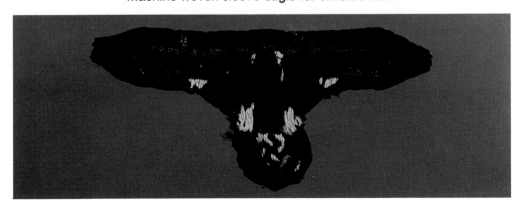

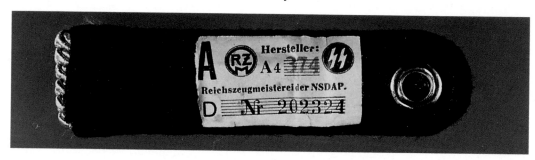

Shoulder cord/board (front and back) worn by ranks of SS-Standartenführer through SS-Oberführer from May 1933 to October 1933 and by ranks of SS-Sturmbannführer through SS-Standartenführer from October 1933 to May 1945.

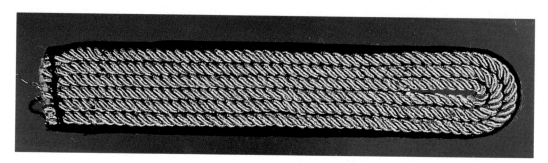

Shoulder cord/board (front and back) worn by ranks of SS-Sturmführer through SS-Obersturmbannführer from May of 1933 to October of 1933 and by ranks of SS-Untersturmführer through SS-Hauptsturmführer from October 1933 to May of 1945.

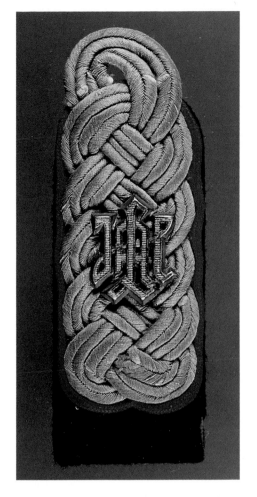

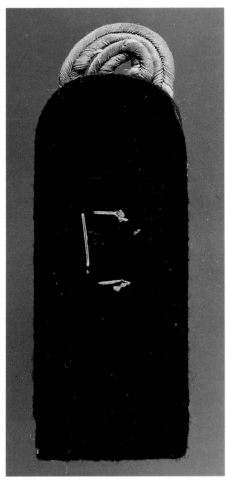

Front and back – shoulder board of an artillery SS–Sturmbannführer of "Leibstandarte SS Adolf Hitler."

Prewar shoulder strap of an SS-Oberscharführer "LAH."

Detail of metal monogram "LAH" for wear on officer's shoulder boards.

Front and back – white metal monogram for NCO shoulder boards of "Der Führer."

SS-Armbadges were introduced to denote specialties and functions. They were usually on a black diamond shaped cloth patch and embroidered in silver bullion for officers and gray thread for enlisted men. Many types of these arm badges exist. Several are provided as original examples.

ABOVE and BELOW: Arm badge for Staff of the SD.

ABOVE and BELOW: Arm badge for SS-Verwaltungsführer or Administrative Leader.

ABOVE and BELOW: Arm badge for an officer assigned to Staff of the SS-Main Race and Rehabilitation Office.

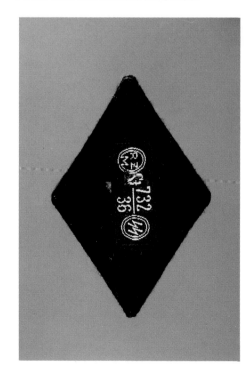

 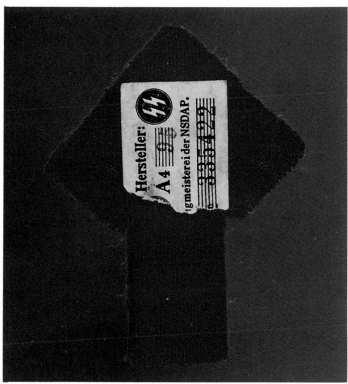

This arm badge, worn on the upper left arm, was for graduates of the Leadership School (Reichsführerschulen).

The SS-Kampfbinde (brassard) was worn on the upper left sleeve of the Allgemeine service uniform. These are commonly called "armbands." The SS armband was the same pattern as the N.S.D.A.P. armband with the addition of black bands at the top and bottom. Note the oval shape of the white disc, typical of SS-Brassards. Brassards on overcoats were normally wider by 1/2 inch than those on uniform tunics. RIGHT: RZM tag on reverse of SS-Brassard.

Front and back – a second example of an SS-Brassard with markings of "Leibstandarte Adolf Hitler." This is an early example dating from the 1933 to 1935 period.

Honor Chevron for ex-members of the Police and Armed Forces.

The cloth Sports insignia was worn on numerous athletic garments. This example (black runes on white disc) is the second pattern. The first pattern had the colors reversed.

Five men in this photograph are wearing the 1st pattern Sports insignia. The man center, first row, wears the second pattern.

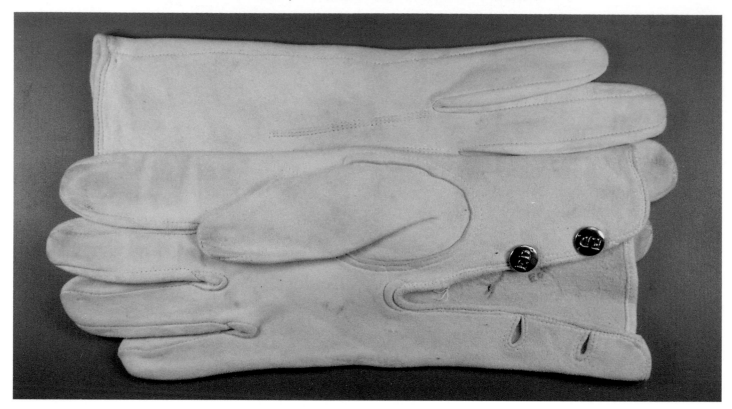

Dress Gloves

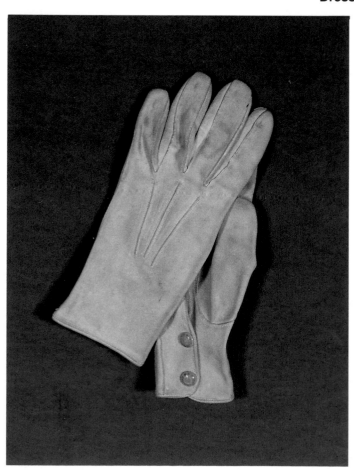

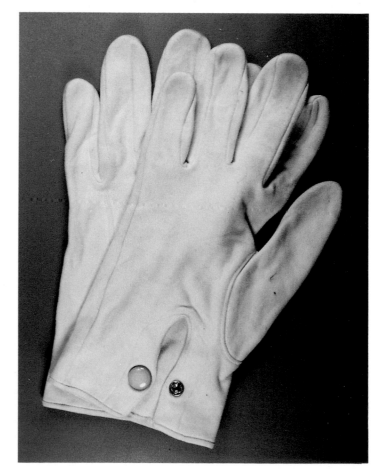

Boots

SS Officer's Boots.

Spur in position on SS officer's boot.

RIGHT: Small SS runes can be seen stamped in the leather inside.

The four officers around the car are wearing boots similar to those on page 81.

SS dress boots.

Sole of SS dress boot.

SS markings stamped inside boots.

SS field boots. This pair has reflectors strapped around the ankles.

Cloth tag sewn inside field boots.

These men are wearing similar pattern field boots.

Belts and Buckles

The SS enlisted belt and buckle.

Detail of catch on enlisted belt.

The enlisted belt and buckle in white.

Markings on white enlisted belt.

The following are three examples, front and back, of SS enlisted belt buckles. Note the different markings visible on the backs.

The officer's dress belt for wear with the black uniform.

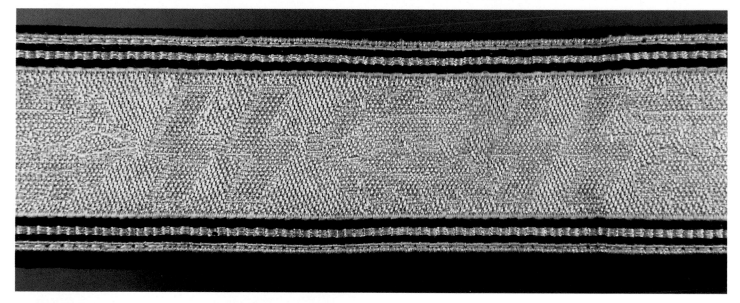

ABOVE: Detail of belt. Note SS runes woven into the design.

Reverse of officer's buckle.

This dress belt, bordered in field grey, was for wear with the field grey uniform. RIGHT: Reverse of officer's buckle.

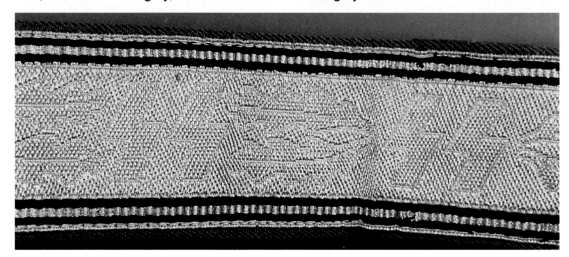

Detail of belt.

Front and back – another example of the officer's belt buckle.

This period publication features an SS officer's buckle on the cover.

The open claw style buckle.

Buckle on a shoulder strap.

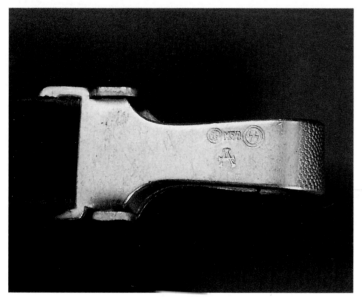

SS markings on the reverse of a shoulder strap clip.

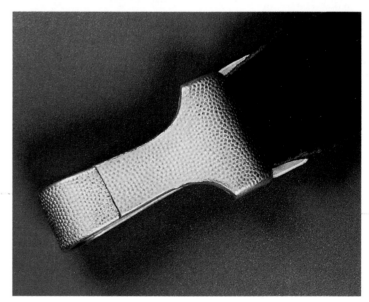

Front side of shoulder strap clip.

Markings on shoulder strap.

Leather belts and shoulder straps are worn by these SS troops on parade.

Other examples of markings on SS belts.

CHAPTER 2

HEADGEAR

Early Allgemeine SS enlisted man's visor hat.

Interior view with maker's markings.

A second variation of an early Allgemeine SS enlisted visor hat.

Interior view with SS markings and owner's name.

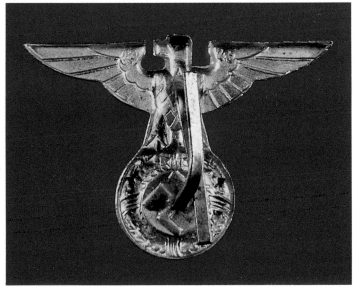

Front and back of 1st pattern hat eagle.

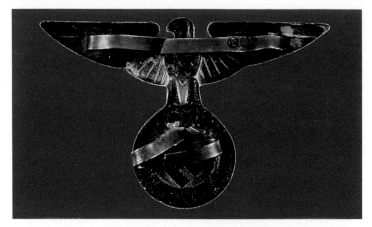

Another variation of the first pattern hat eagle-front and back.

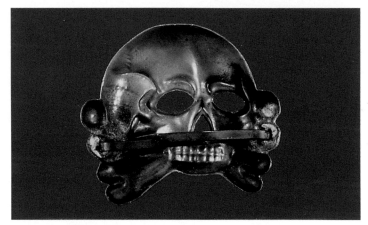

Front and back of first pattern hat skull device.

Allgemeine SS troops wearing the early style enlisted visor hat.

Later version of the Allgemeine SS enlisted visor hat.

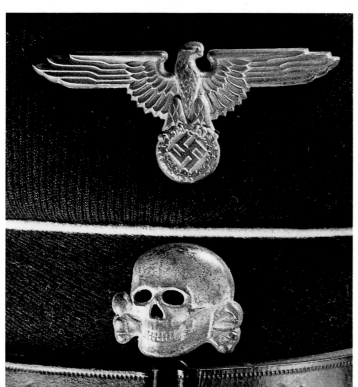

ABOVE: Interior detail with SS markings and owner's name.

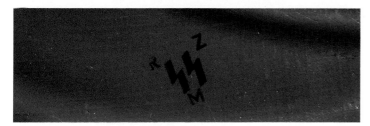

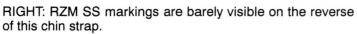

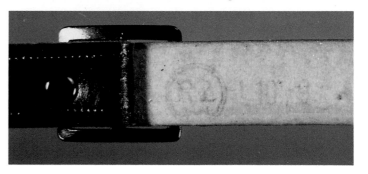

ABOVE: RZM SS markings on visor.

RIGHT: RZM SS markings are barely visible on the reverse of this chin strap.

Allgemeine SS officer's visor hat.

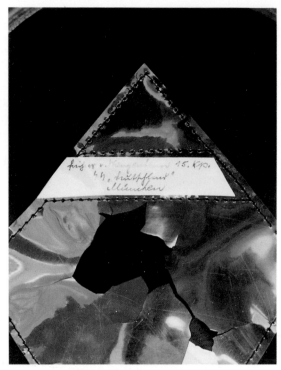

Interior view of the hat at left.

This officer (right) wears the black visor hat with early style eagle.

ABOVE, BELOW and OPPOSITE PAGE: Another variation of the Allge-meine SS officer's visor hat. This example is unissued.

ABOVE: Interior with size 56 marking in place.

RZM SS stamp on visor.

The visor hat, as worn by an officer of SS-Standarte "Germania."

The sweat band is unstitched in this hat, which allows us to clearly view the tag inside.

SS UNIFORMS, INSIGNIA & ACCOUTREMENTS

The visor hat of a General officer of the Allgemeine SS.

Detail of reverse of side button.

WAFFEN-SS OFFICER'S VISOR HATS

This example shows a lot of wear, but is a fine, honest example.

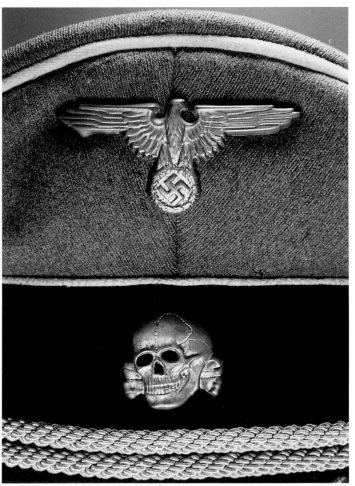

Yet another example of the Waffen SS officer's visor, is this piece marked "Extra" on the sweatband.

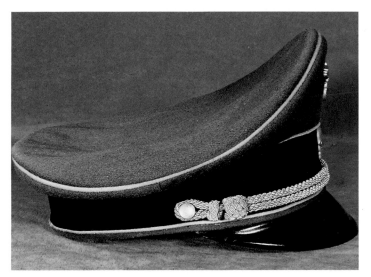 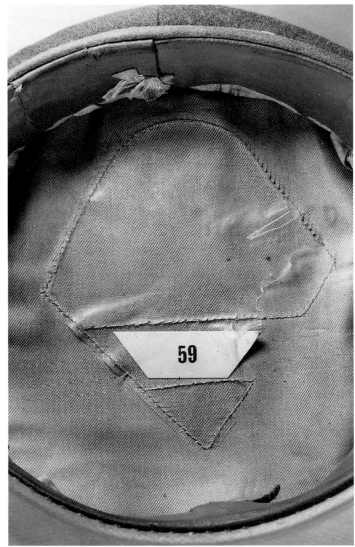

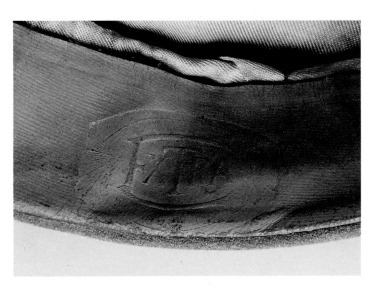

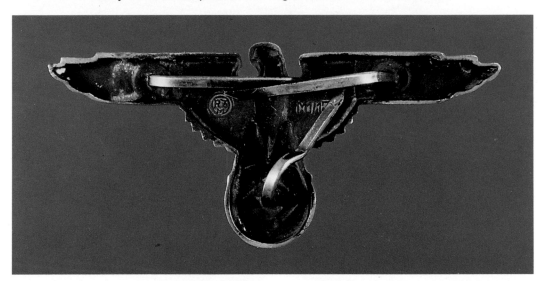

Early war second pattern hat eagle in silver – front and back.

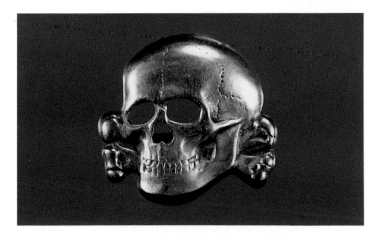

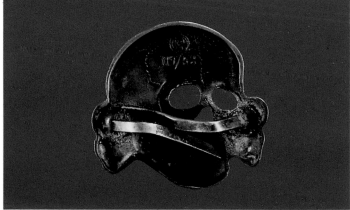

Early war second pattern hat skull device in silver – front and back.

Late war, white metal hat eagle – front and back.

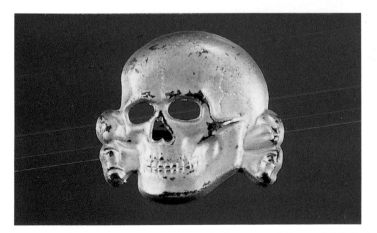

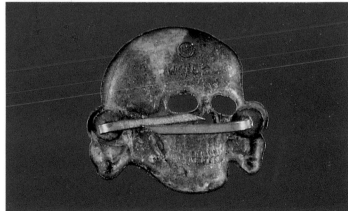

Late war, white metal hat skull device – front and back.

THE SS-FELDMUTZEN (Field Cap)

This first pattern SS field cap originated in the Imperial German Army. It was worn early on by the SS and original examples are very rare today.

Early SS-Feldmutzen.

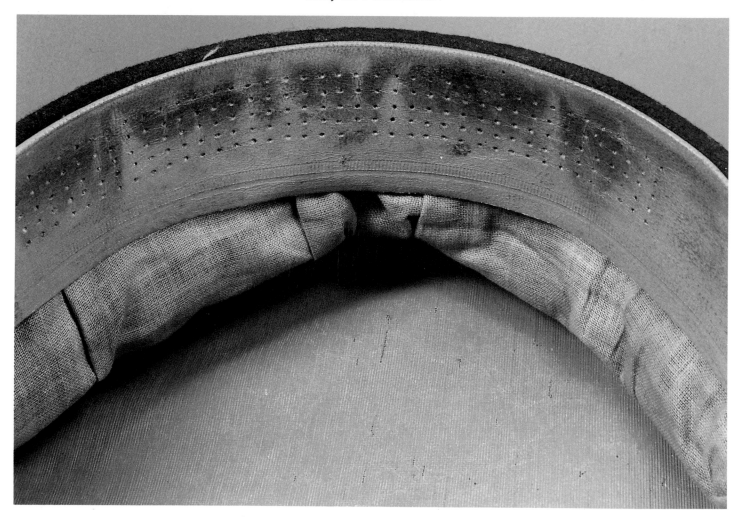

Detail of sweat band and interior lining fabric.

Detail of insignia.

Detail of interior markings. Note 1933 date.

ABOVE and NEXT PAGE: Examples of the early Feldmutzen being worn.

ABOVE: Later version of the SS-Feldmutze.

RIGHT: Feldmutze insignia.

BELOW: Feldmutze label.

Feldmutze for armored personnel.

RIGHT: Insignia detail.

This man wears the Waffen-SS Feld-mutze in field grey.

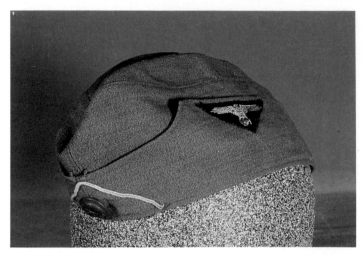

The model 1938 Waffen-SS field cap. The white inverted chevron (soutache) indicates infantry.

Detail of SS eagle.

The soutache was threaded through a small slit in the cloth and stitched in place at the base on each side. This photograph shows the back side.

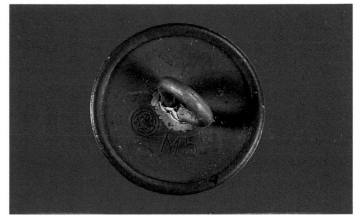

Front and back of cap button.

These SS recruits are wearing field caps.

Front and back of a well worn SS field cap eagle.

Bullion eagle for officer's cap.

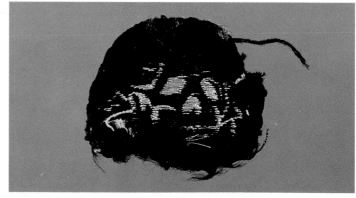

Front and back of cloth SS skull for wear on the field cap.

The Waffen-SS 1943 general issue field cap or Einheitsfeldmutze (commonly called the M-43).

Insignia details Waffen-SS 1943 general issue field cap.

Several variations of SS headgear are visible in this photograph.

CHAPTER 2: HEADGEAR

The RZM model SS steel helmet was worn prior to 1931 without decals. It was very similar in appearance to the model 1916 German helmet. It is interesting to note that these helmets are actually dark blue not black.

The RZM model SS steel helmet.

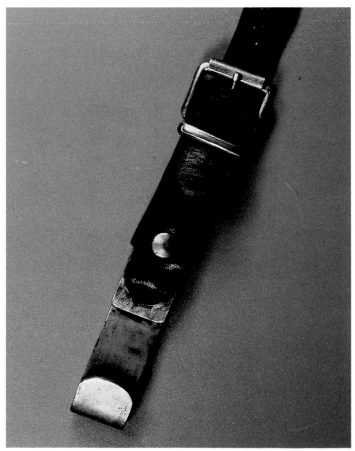

ABOVE: Interior view.

RIGHT: Chin strap detail.

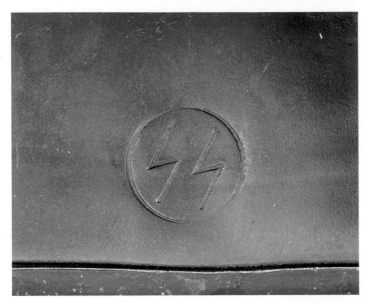

Markings inside RZM model SS helmet shown on page 113.

LEFT: The RZM model SS steel helmet worn by this standard bearer. Also of interest is the standard bearer's gorget around his neck. RIGHT: These men are holding the RZM model helmet.

ALLGEMEINE SS M35 STEEL HELMET

Left side decal on the Allgemeine SS M35 helmet.

Right side decal on the Allgemeine SS M35 helmet.

Interior markings on the Allgemeine SS M35 helmet.

Interior view.

Original owner's name inked in liner.

Interior markings.

Right side decal on the Waffen-SS M35 helmet.

Left side decal on the Waffen-SS M35 helmet.

ABOVE and OPPOSITE: Waffen SS troops wearing the M35 helmet.

Decal detail.

RIGHT: Interior markings.

CHAPTER 2: HEADGEAR
PARATROOPER HELMET WITH WAFFEN SS SNIPER (VEIL)

This helmet was "liberated" by an American soldier at the Battle of the Bulge. The camouflage, wire, and veil were in place as seen here.

Right side metal insignia.

Left side metal insignia.

CHAPTER 3

FIELD GEAR & EQUIPMENT

THE SS BACKPACK

Backpack as viewed from the rear with mess tin and folded ground sheet in place.

Backpack with shoulder straps visible. BELOW: SS and RZM markings stamped into leather.

RIGHT: Inside of pack. Note SS label in center.

BELOW: SS man wearing the backpack with field gray uniform.

SS FIELD MEDICAL KIT

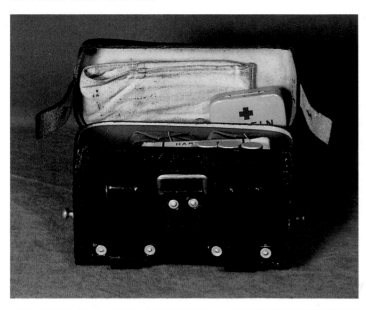

Markings on medical kit.

SS BREAD BAG AND CANTEEN (BEFORE 1936)

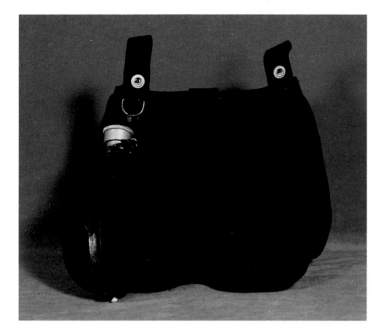

ABOVE: Tag found inside bag. BELOW: SS markings on bag.

SS markings on neck of canteen.

SS markings on cap of canteen.

Front and back of map case.

Markings stamped into leather map case.

RIGHT: This SS officer is carrying a map case similar to the example pictured.

SS REFLECTORS FOR WEAR AT NIGHT ON TRAFFIC DUTY

ABOVE: Reflectors and case. BELOW LEFT: Detail of back of link with SS runes stamped in. RIGHT: Reflectors and chain detail.

BINOCULARS AND CASE

LEFT: Binoculars on case with owner's name and runes on leather lens cover. RIGHT: SS officer in the field with binoculars around his neck.

SS TENT PEGS AND CASE

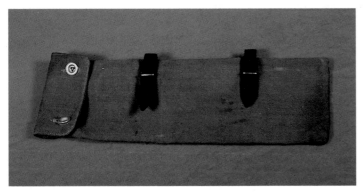

ABOVE: Tent peg case. BELOW: SS markings and tag in case.

SS markings, stamped into tent pegs.

CHAPTER 4
FIREARMS

Luger "Black Widow", 41 dated byf (Mauser).

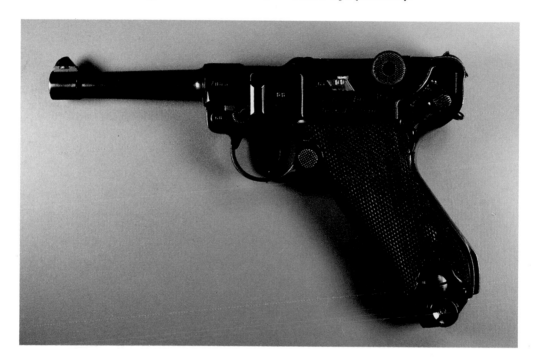

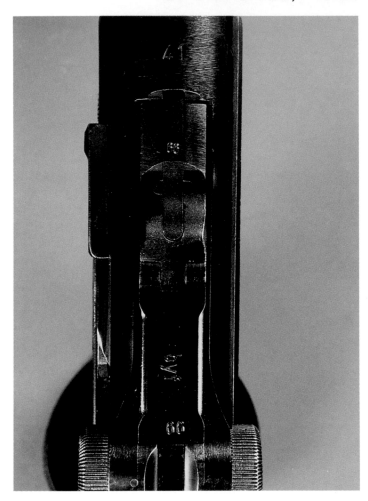

SS motto "Meine Ehre Heisst Treue" inscribed above grip. This gun was likely given as a token of friendship or as an award.

Luger, 1940-42 code "Totenkopf" (Death's Head)

Examples of lugers marked with the Totenkopf insignia are very rare. This gun was probably assigned to a concentration camp guard.

Note runes and Totenkopf stamped above grip.

Runes and Totenkopf can be seen above 1940 date.

SS UNIFORMS, INSIGNIA & ACCOUTREMENTS

Luger, 41/42 code Mauser with double strike SS runes.

This pistol is a very unusual example which was acquired from a U.S. Army veteran of the 2nd Armored Division. It has been speculated that the double strike SS runes were put on the gun by an SS technician at the time of a rework or repair. All numbers match including the clip.

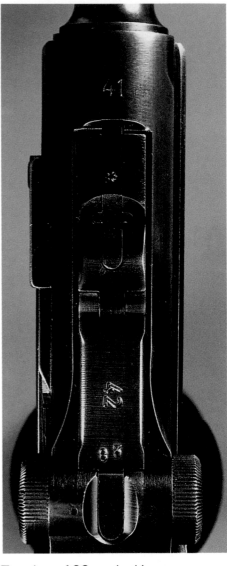

Top view of SS marked Luger.

Partial rune stamp is visible in front of the three eagle markings.

The rune stamps are again visible in front of the 9683 number.

Detail of markings.

SS men on the pistol range practicing with the Luger.

AC41 Code P.38 "Totenkopf" (Death's Head).

Very few examples of Totenkopf marked P.38 pistols are known to exist. These guns were likely issued to concentration camp guards.

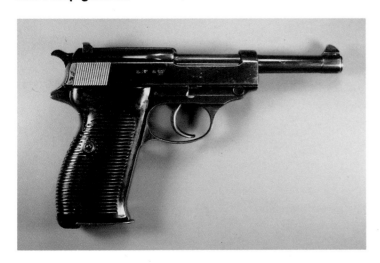 

Note matching number on clip.

"Death's Head" stamp detail.

Unusual pigskin P.38 holster attributed to an SS Oberscharführer Wittman.

Detail of nametag inside holster flap.

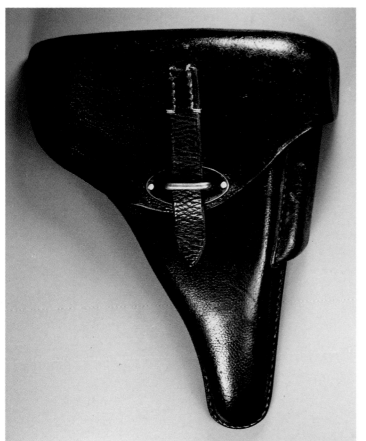

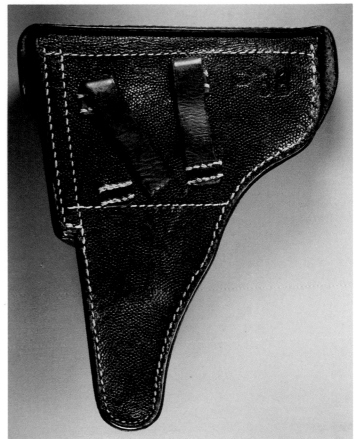

Model 35 Polish Radom automatic pistol issued to a Waffen SS soldier.

ABOVE: SS markings inside Radom holster.

LEFT: Model 35 Radom holster.

Sauer .32 pistol and holster as preferred by many SS officers. The Sauer .32 was the only pistol designed, produced, and used during the period of the Third Reich.

SS markings on stock of training rifle.

BELOW: .22 Mauser training rifle with SS markings.

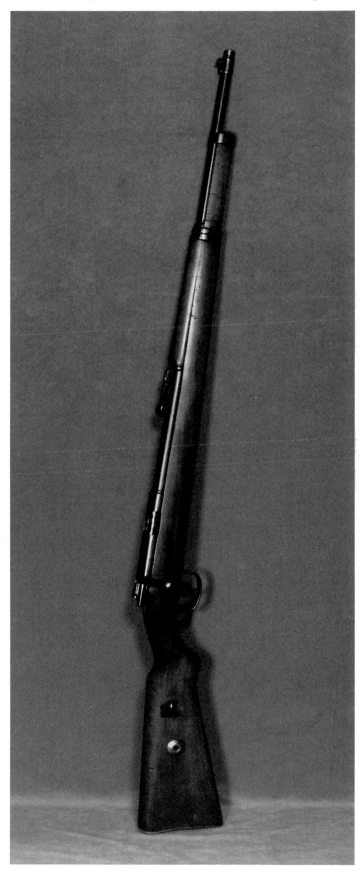

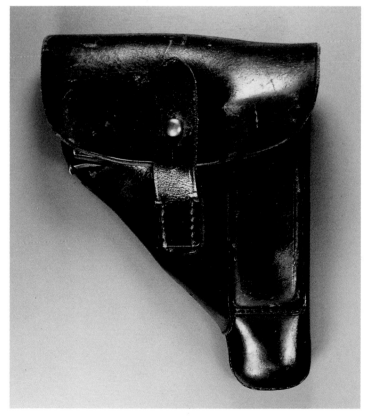

ABOVE: Leather holster for the Sauer .32

CHAPTER 5
EDGED WEAPONS

The 1933 SS service dagger made by Robert Klaas with vertical leather hanger.

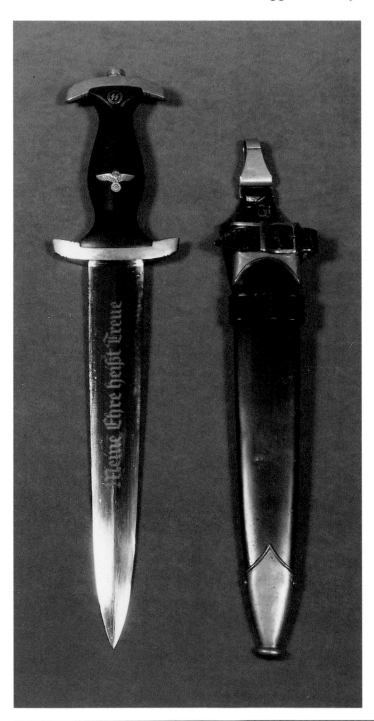

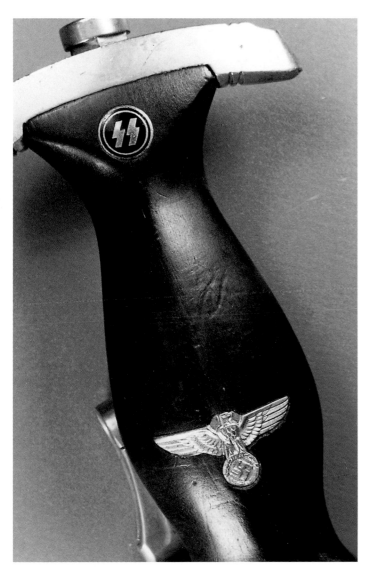

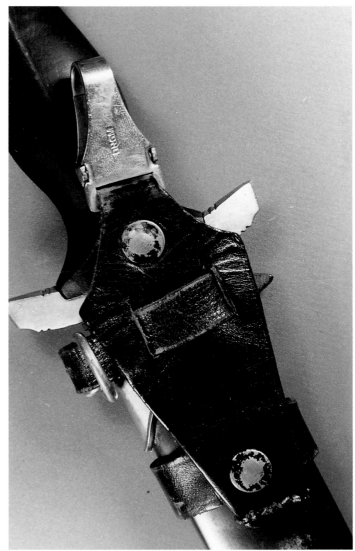

The 1933 SS service dagger by Gottlieb Hammesfahr.

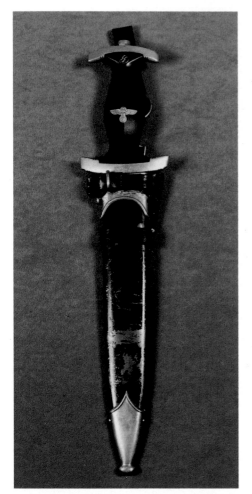

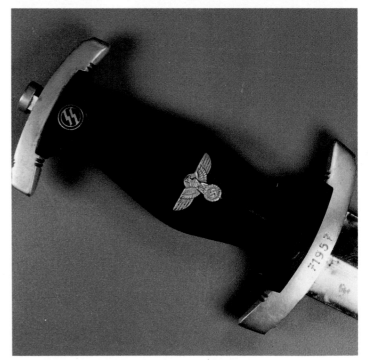

Gottlieb Hammesfahr maker's mark.

Grip detail.

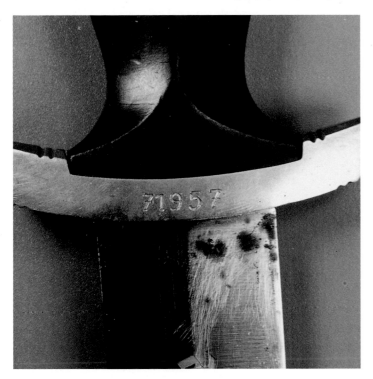

SS number stamped into crossguard.

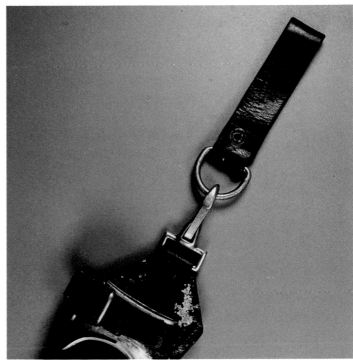

Hanger detail.

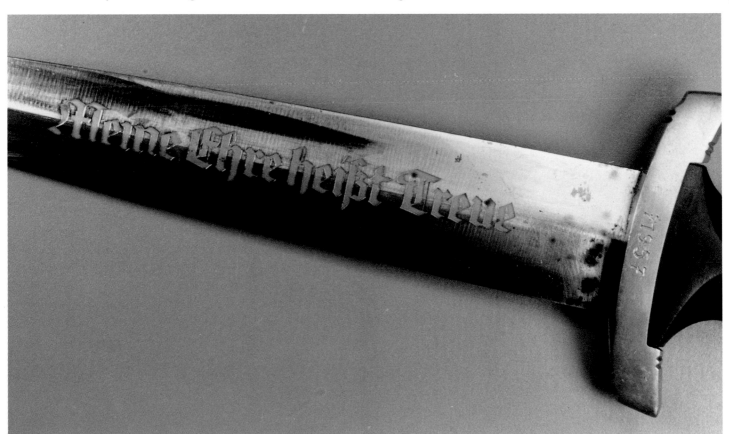

Blade inscription.

The 1933 SS service dagger by Boker.

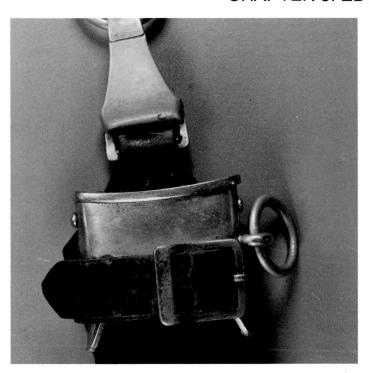

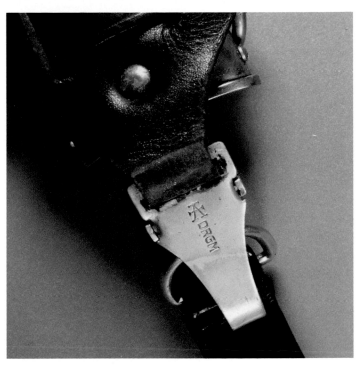

The 1933 SS service dagger - later "RZM" variation.

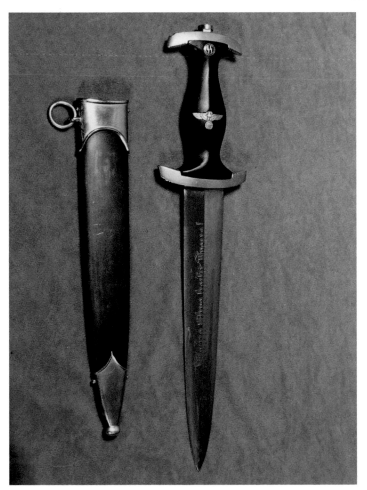

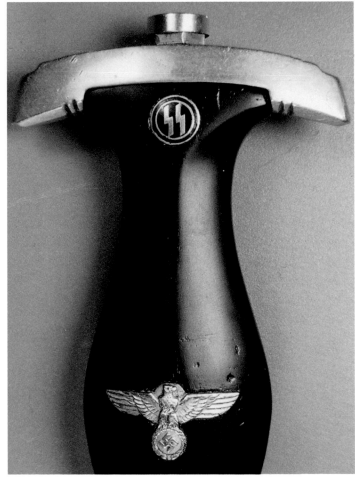

The SS Rohm Honor Dagger with ground inscription.

In 1934, 9,900 SS members were awarded the "Rohm Honor Dagger." The blade was inscribed "In herzlicher freundschaft Ernst Rohm" (In heartfelt friendship Ernst Rohm). When Rohm was murdered, the inscription was ordered removed. A "Rohm Honor Dagger" with inscription intact is probably the most difficult SS dagger to find today.

ABOVE: Inscription on front side of blade. BELOW: Reverse of blade with ground inscription. On careful examination, portions of the inscription are visible. "Ground Rohm" daggers are seldom found todayt.

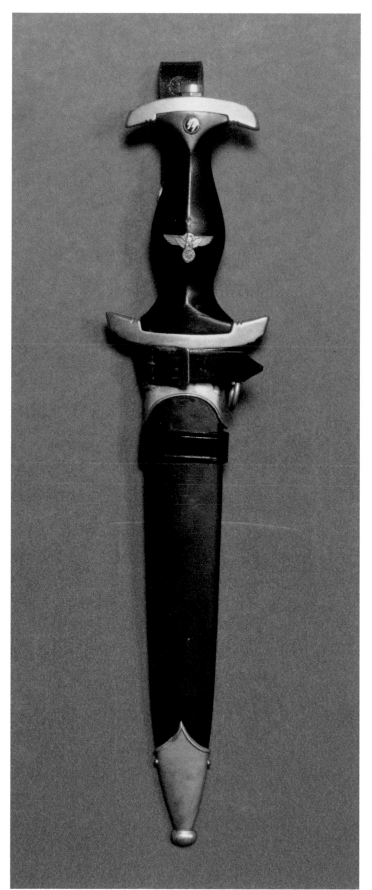

Carl Eickhorn maker's mark.

The blade of a Rohm Honor Dagger with inscription still present, made by Gottlieb Hammesfahr. *(Henger)*

Detail of inscription. *(Henger)*

Detail of Rohm signature. *(Henger)*

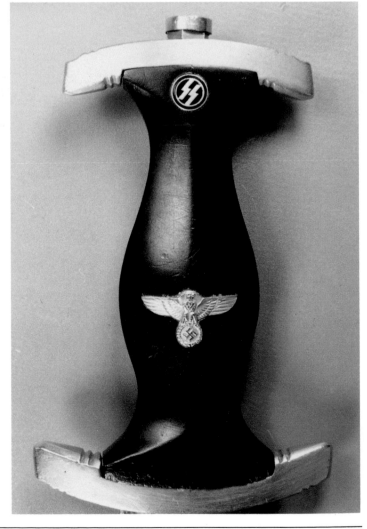

Maker's mark. *(Henger)*

RIGHT: Detail of grip. *(Henger)*

A second un-ground Rohm example is this blade by Eickhorn. *(Henger)*

Detail of Rohm signature. *(Henger)*

Detail of Eickhorn maker's mark. Note SS man's number stamped into crossguard. *(Henger)*

SS UNIFORMS, INSIGNIA & ACCOUTREMENTS

SS Himmler Honor Dagger

This is one of the most rare and sought after SS daggers today. Heinrich Himmler presented these pieces to members of the squads who carried out the assassinations of Rohm and other SA leaders. The inscription on the blade reads "In herzlicher freundschaft, H. Himmler" ("In heartfelt friendship, H. Himmler"). These daggers were all made by Eickhorn.

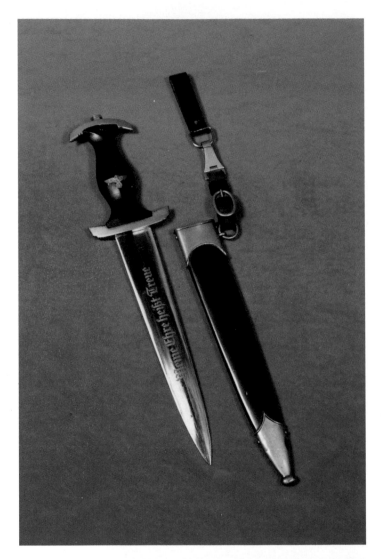
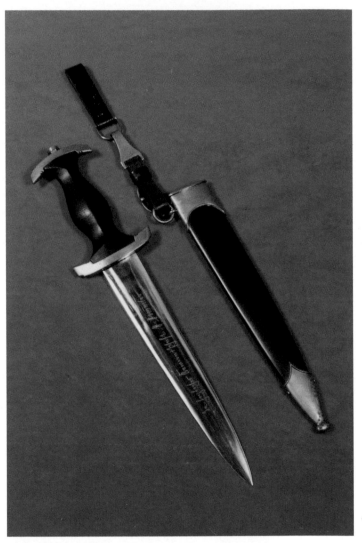

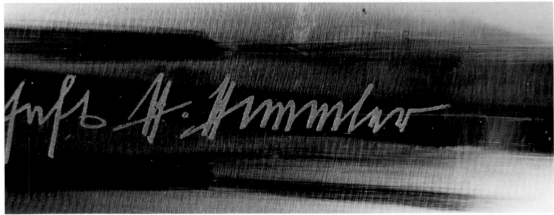

Detail of "H. Himmler" signature inscription.

Reverse of blade with inscription.

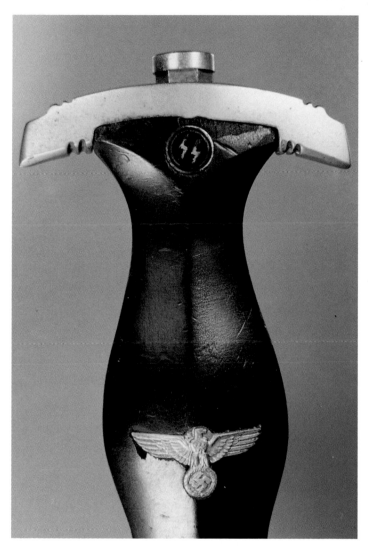

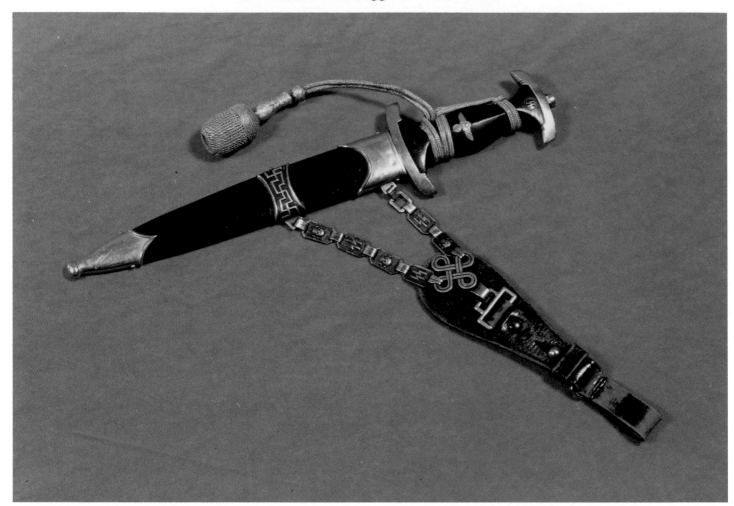

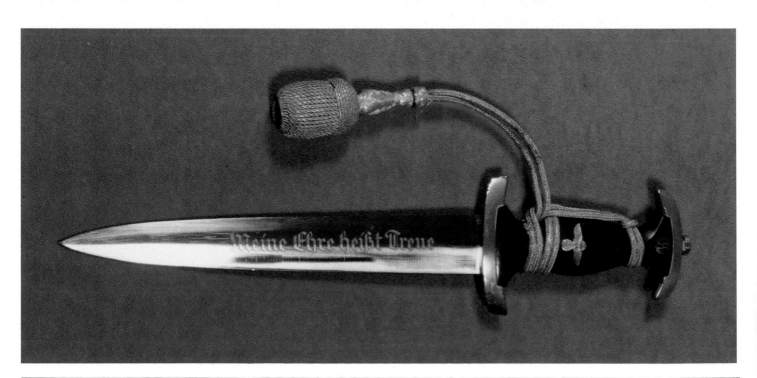

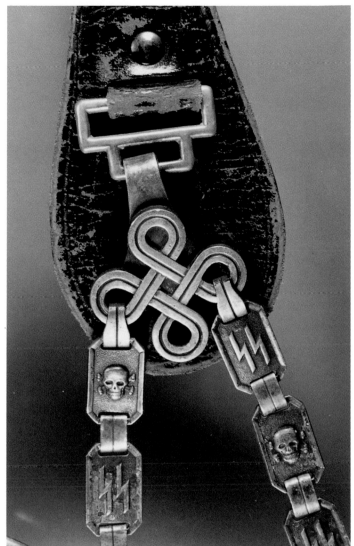

Detail of Type II chain and hanger attachment. Note the beveled connectors where the chain hooks to the cloverleaf.

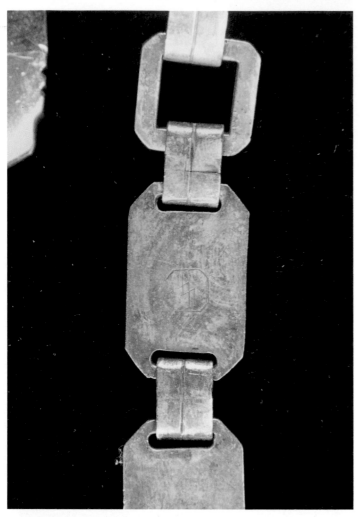

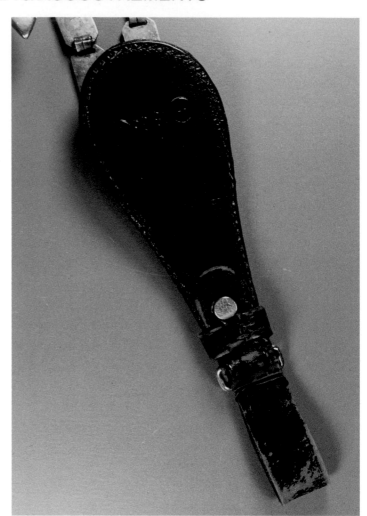

SS proof marks on Type II chain.

Reverse of leather hanger.

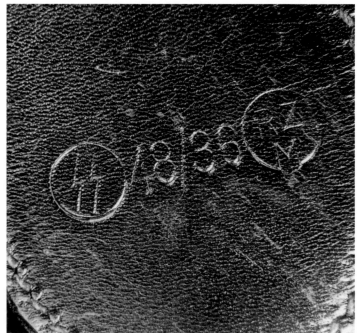

SS/RZM proof stamps on leather hanger.

1936 model SS dagger as worn with uniform coat.

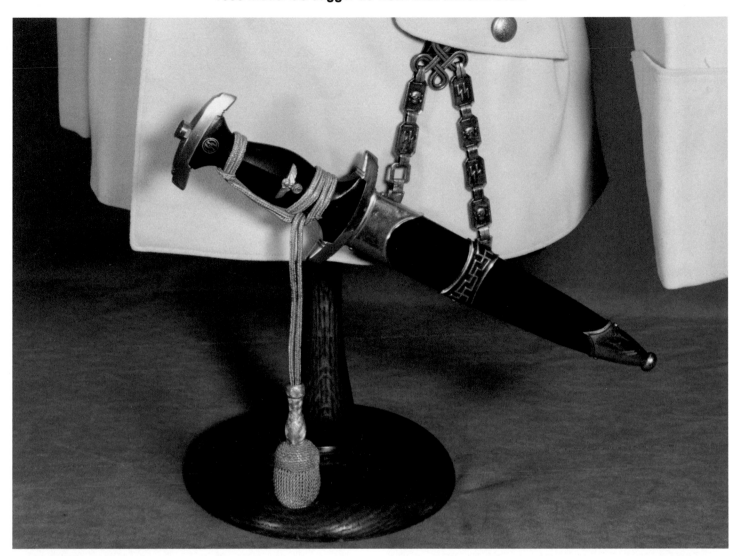

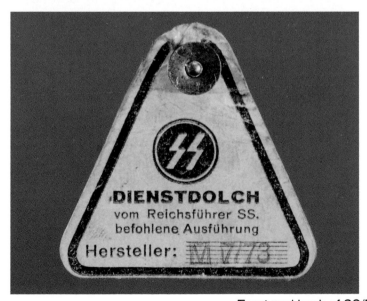

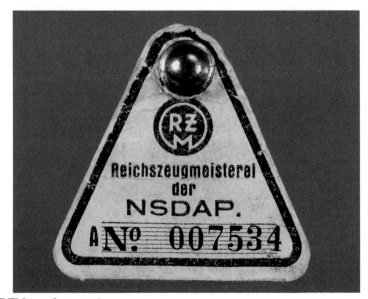

Front and back of SS/RZM tag from a dagger.

Dress bayonet and SS troddle (knot).

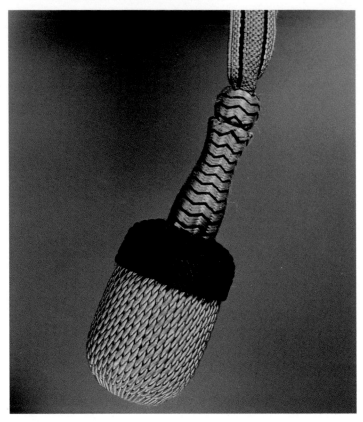

Detail of troddle.

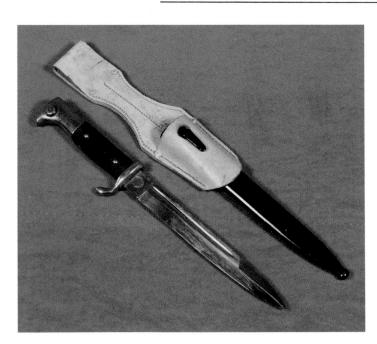

Dress bayonet with rare white leather frog.

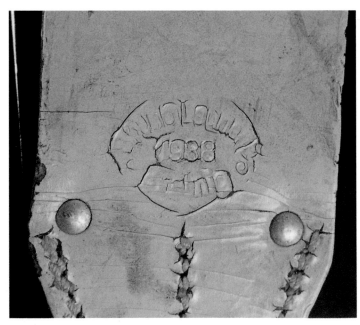

Markings and 1938 date stamped into leather.

CHAPTER 5: EDGED WEAPONS

The Himmler Presentation Damascus steel letter opener.

(Although not an edged weapon, this seems the most appropriate location in this work for this piece. These Damascus steel letter openers are very rare.)

Front and back of Himmler presentation letter opener shown here on top of the leather presentation case.

"H. Himmler" signature detail.

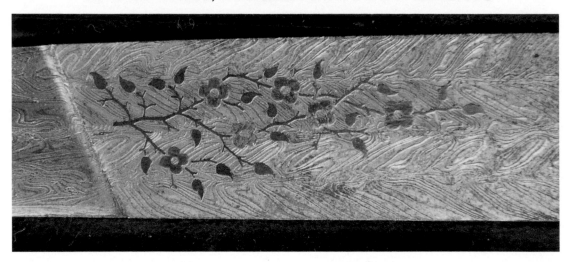

Detail of flower design on opposite side.

Detail of point.

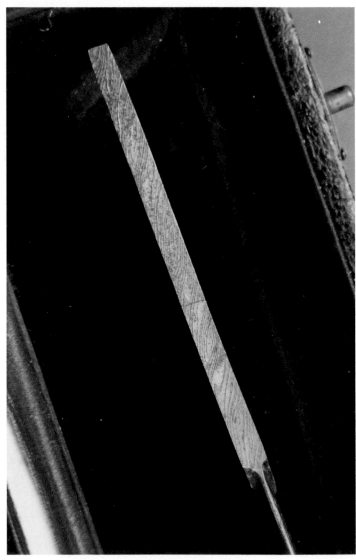

The Damascus work is also very apparent on the edge of the piece.

CHAPTER 5: EDGED WEAPONS

SS Swords (Degens)

A mounted SS officer in the field with sword drawn.

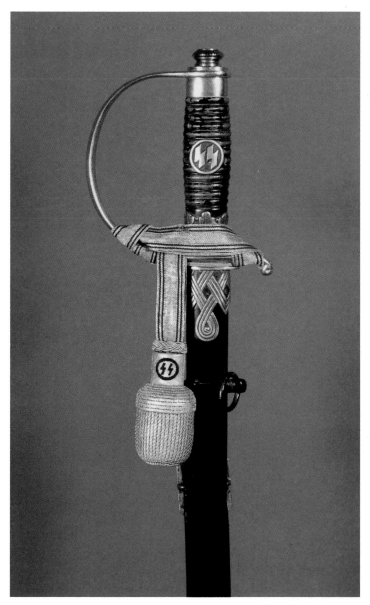
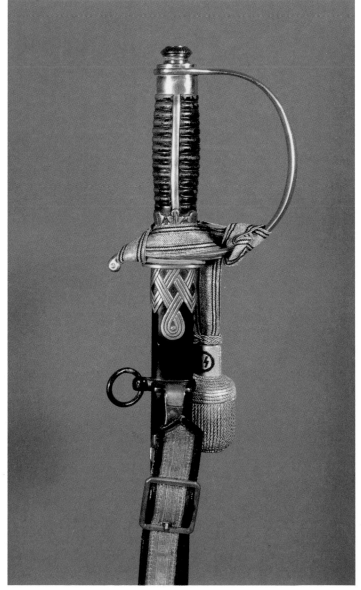

The SS officer's sword with portepee.

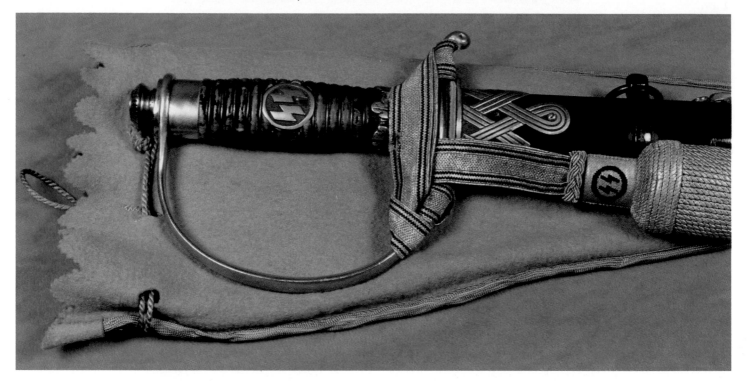

Detail of SS officer's sword and portopee laying on top of cloth storage bag.

Detail of runes in well worn grip.

Reverse of grip.

Detail of white leather washer and SS proofs in crossguard.

Pommel of officer's sword.

Throat of scabbard with SS proof marks.

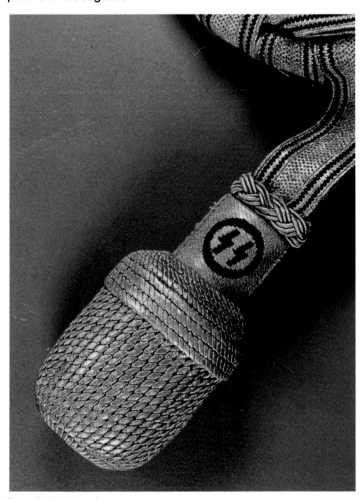

Detail of officer's portepee.

Cloth RZM/SS issue tag on portepee.

RIGHT: An SS officer with his sword.

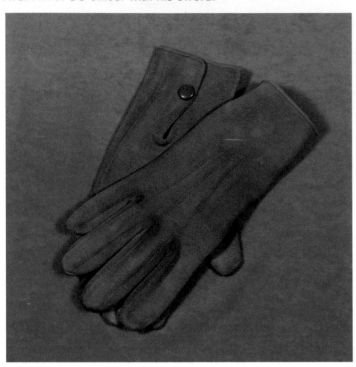

The officer in the photograph at right wears these grey dress gloves.

The SS Officer Candidate Leader pattern sword and portepee.

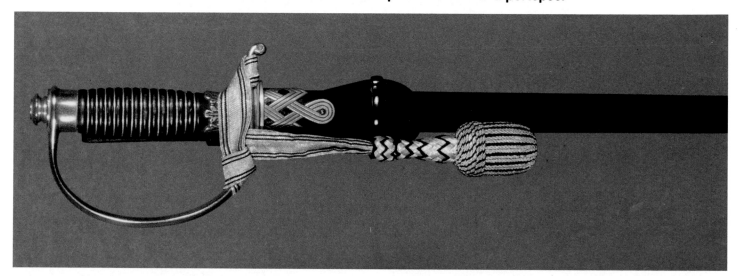

Note leather washer.

WKC maker's markings.

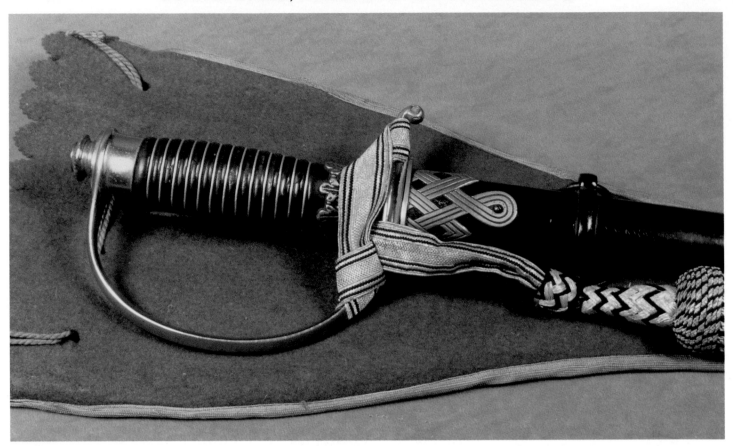

Detail of Officer Candidate Leader pattern sword laying on cloth storage bag.

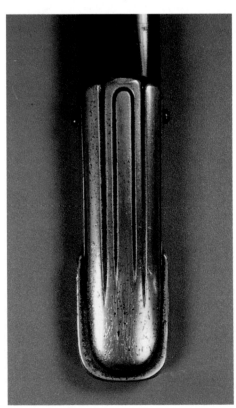

Pommel.

Detail of drag.

Detail of portepee.

The SS NCO sword and portepee.

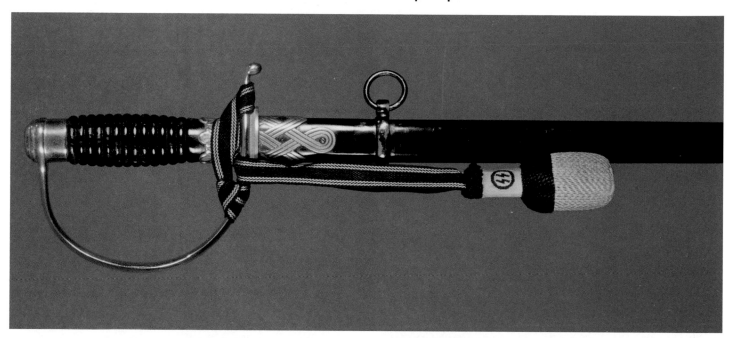

Note leather washer.

Maker's markings of F.W. Holler.

LEFT: Grip detail.

BELOW: Pommel.

BELOW: Scabbard throat with SS proofs.

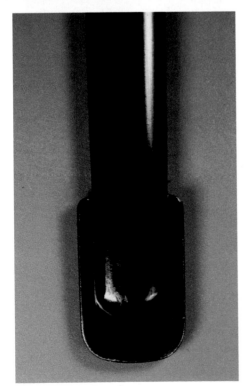

Drag.

Note SS proofs in leather hanger.

Detail of portepee.

The SS Police Officer's sword and portepee.

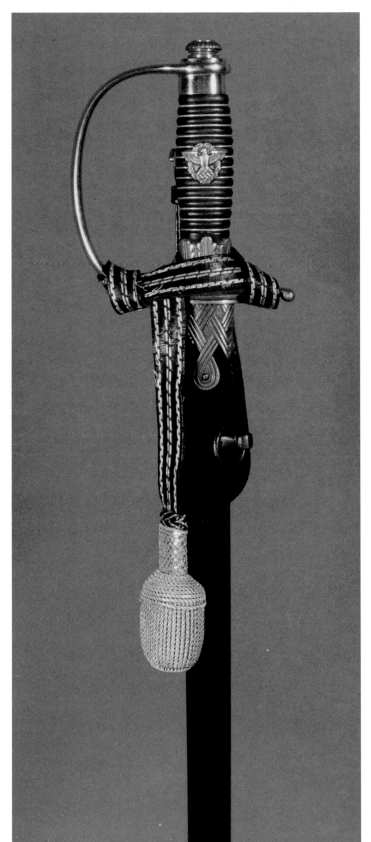

Front and back of SS Police Officer's sword with portepee and hanger in place.

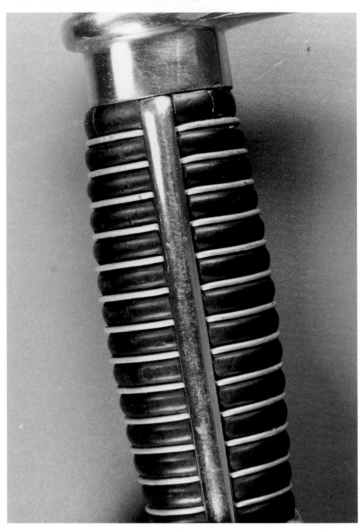

Detail of grip.

Back side of grip.

Pommel.

Note SS marking on crossguard.

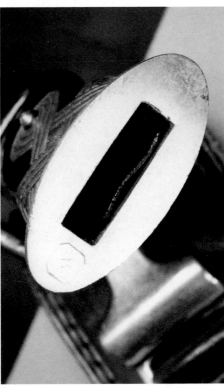

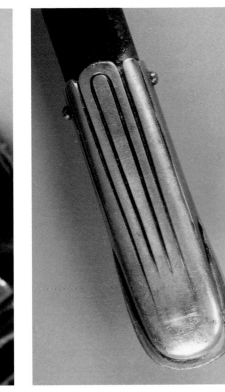

Eickhorn maker's markings.

Scabbard throat with SS proofs.

Detail of drag.

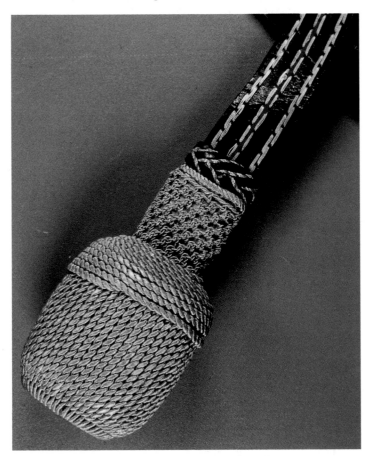

Portepee details.

Hangers

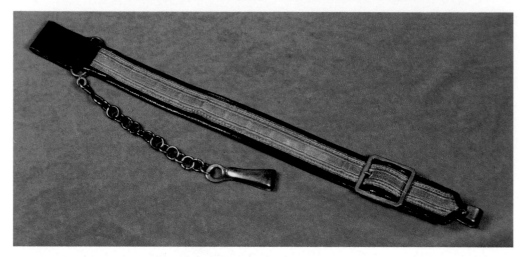

Hanger for the SS sword.

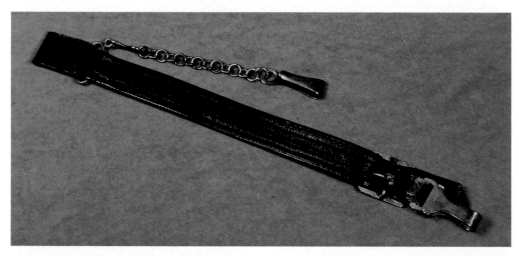

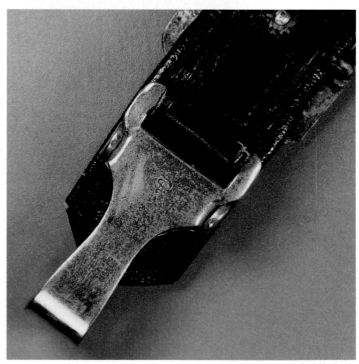

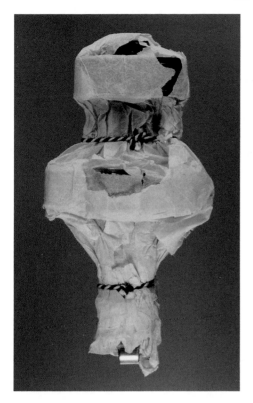

Vertical hanger for 1933 model SS dagger in original wrap.

Two examples of leather vertical hangers for the 1933 model SS dagger. Note RZM/SS markings barely visible in the leather.

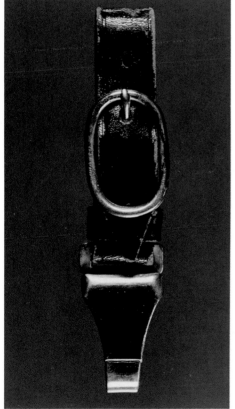

Front and back of diagonal style leather hanger for the 1933 model SS dagger.

Belt attachment for dagger hanger. Note RZM/SS markings.

CHAPTER 6

MEDALS AND BADGES

The medals and badges awarded to the Waffen SS were, for the most part, the same ones awarded to the Army. Many political awards were also common to the SA. An in-depth study of medals and badges of the SS is much too broad a topic for the scope of this work, but I wanted the reader to have access to a photographic overview of the subject.

The Golden Party Decoration and Badge

On the 30th of January, annually, most Golden Party badges were given as the highest decoration of the party. Each was dated and marked with initials A.H.

Front and back – the Golden Party Decoration. This example, dated 30, January 1943, has a war time replacement pin, which covers the A.H. markings. Note, also, lettering on face of badge is gilt.

Front and back – standard issue Golden Party Badge.

The Golden Party Badge was also given to members of the N.S.D.A.P. with solid service records and membership numbers less than 100,000.

Front and back – this example is a period facsimile for shop window display.

Front and back – N.S.D.A.P. party pin.

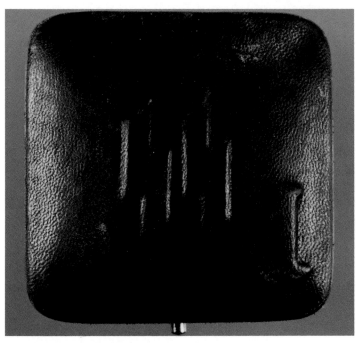

Cased set – Party Badge and Eagle stick pin. Case back is dated 1936, embossed with runes and the numeral one for SS-Standarte "Deutschland."

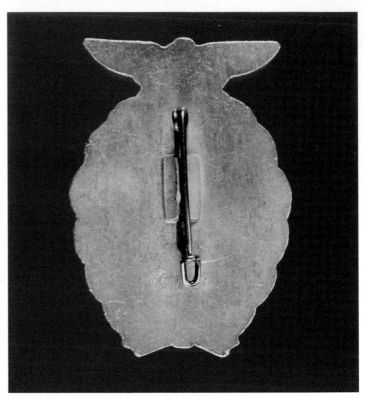

Front and back – S.A. Rally at Brunswick 1931 Badge of Honor.

Nuremburg Badge of Honor 1929 made into a watch fob.

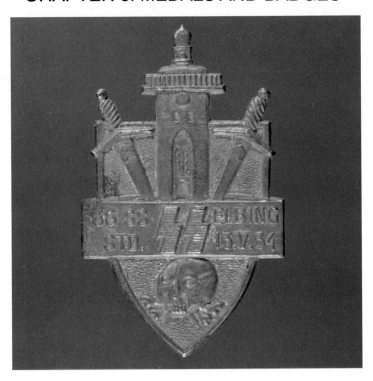

Tinnie: SS Elbing 13.V.34. Building depicted is believed to be rendition of gates to A.H. Division barracks. *(Stairrett)*

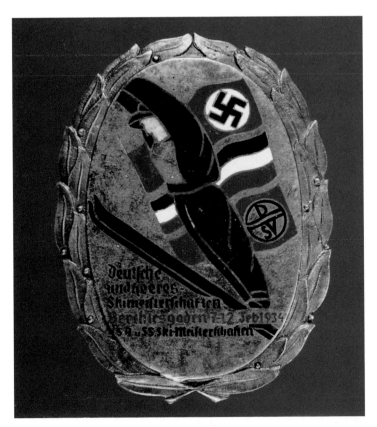 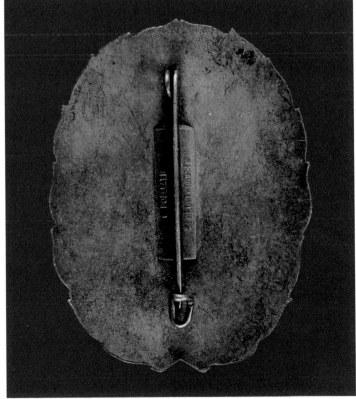

Front and back – 1934 SA-SS Ski Badge.

The Germanic Proficiency Runes Badge. This badge was presented in bronze and silver.

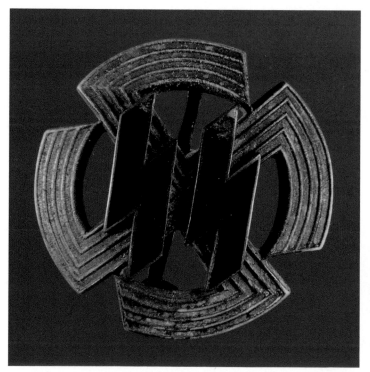

The S.A. Military Sports Badge.

This badge was awarded in three classes – bronze, silver, and gold.

ABOVE: Front and back of the S.A. Military Sports Badge in bronze.

ABOVE: Front and back of the S.A. Military Sports Badge in silver.

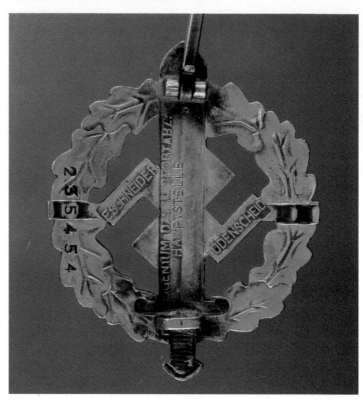

ABOVE: Front and back of the S.A. Military Sports Badge in gold.

The S.A. Military Sports Badge for war wounded.

The German National Badge for Physical Training (last version with swastika). This badge was awarded in bronze, silver and gold.

The SS Civil Badge (SS-Zivilabzeichen) – to be worn on civilian clothes to demonstrate membership in the SS. Note outer ring is thicker than inner ring.

FM Zeitschrift

Monatsschrift der Reichsführung SS für fördernde Mitglieder

4. Folge / 6. Jahrgang
Berlin, 1. Februar 1939

Der Glückwunsch
des Führers

SS-Supporting Member's Badge.

This period document features the SS Supporting Member's Commemorative Badge.

SS Standard (Danzig) stick pin – note the death's head in the center of the swastika.

OPPOSITE: This period publication (1939) displays the SS Supporting Member's Badge on the cover.

Military Awards

The Iron Cross

The Iron Cross is the best known of all German medals. It was first instituted in 1813 by Friedrich-Wilhelm III. By the end of World War II, there were eight classes of the Iron Cross. The classes were: 2nd Class, 1st Class, Knight's Cross, Knight's Cross with Oak Leaves (Eichenlaub), Knight's Cross with Oak Leaves and Swords (Schwerten), Knight's Cross with Oak Leaves, Swords and Diamonds (Brillanten), Knight's Cross with Golden Oak Leaves, Swords and Diamonds and Grand Cross of the Iron Cross. The only Grand Cross awarded in World War II was to Göring for the Battle of France.

Two examples of the Knight's Cross are shown. The first was manufactured by Steinhauer & Luck, Ludenscheid.

Knight's Cross in issue case by Steinhauer & Luck, Ludensheid.

Front and back of Knight's Cross by Steinhauer & Luck, Ludensheid.

Detail of medal with "935 4" marking visible.

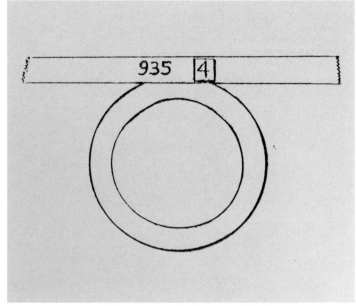

Although not to scale, this drawing illustrates the position of markings in the photo at left.

935 marking is also on the suspension ring.

Ritterkreuz

des

Eisernen

kreuzes

ABOVE and BELOW: Knight's Cross issue box with Steinhauer & Luck, Ludenscheid markings on the end.

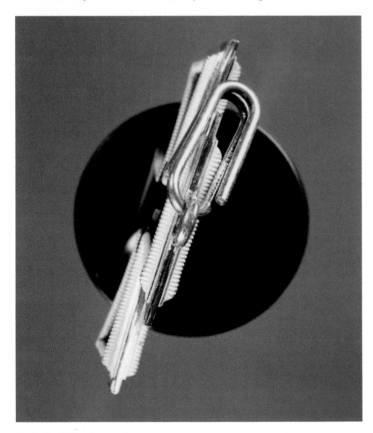

Detail of the top edge.

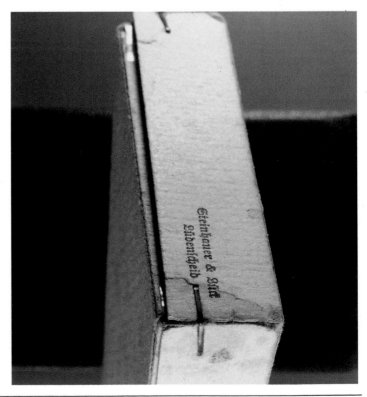

The second Knight's Cross example is marked "800." It could have been made by C.E. Juncker-Berlin, Deschler & Sohn-Munich, or Steinhauer & Luck-Ludenscheid.

Note "800" under ring.

The Oak Leaves

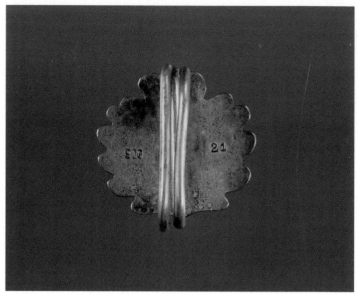

The Oak Leaves and Swords

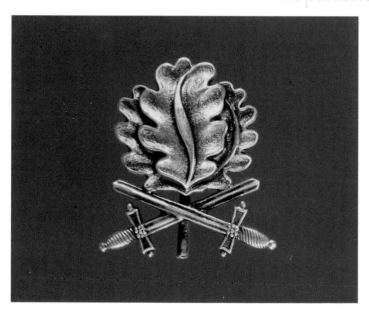
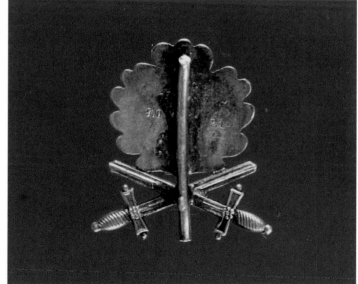

The ring has been clipped off of this example.

The Iron Cross First Class

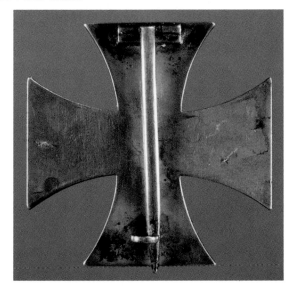

Front and back – this example is a First World War Iron Cross First Class. Many World War I veterans wore this medal on their SS uniforms in the pre-World War II years. The World War II issue medal was identical in appearance except it had a swastika in the center and "1939" at the bottom. The Imperial Crown was also removed.

The Iron Cross Second Class

World War II example as issued.

World War I example with 25 year cluster.

SS UNIFORMS, INSIGNIA & ACCOUTREMENTS

The German Cross

The German Cross was instituted September 28, 1941 to bridge the gap between the Iron Cross First Class and the Knight's Cross. It was awarded in gold to combatants and in silver to recognize distinction in military leadership – not in the face of the enemy.

Front and back – The German Cross in gold.

Front and back – stick pin of the German Cross in gold.

Front and back — the German Cross in silver.

Front and back — stick pin of the German Cross in silver.

SS UNIFORMS, INSIGNIA & ACCOUTREMENTS

1939 Bar to 1914 Iron Cross (Spange)

This bar was awarded to recipients of the Iron Cross in the First World War who were awarded the same grade again in World War II. The Bar or Spange was awarded in 1st and 2nd class.

The 2nd Class Bar in issue box – front and back.

The War Merit Cross

The War Merit Cross was instituted to recognize war effort contributions other than in battle. It was awarded in five grades: Bronze War Merit Medal, Second Class Bronze Cross, First Class Silver Cross, Silver Knight's Cross and Gold Knight's Cross. Each grade was awarded with swords (for military contributions) or without swords (for contributions such as propaganda, administration, etc.). Only two classes of this decoration are shown.

Knight's Cross in silver with swords.

Note "900" mark on edge.

Front and back detail.

The Knight's Cross in silver without swords.

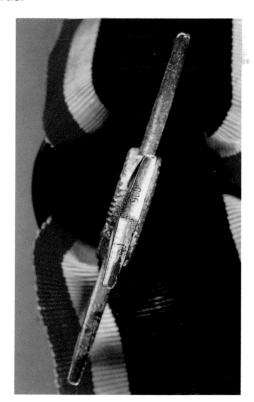

The Wounded Badge

The Wounded Badge was awarded in three classes: Black (for one or two wounds), silver (for three or four wounds) and in gold (for Five or more wounds). The silver could be awarded for loss of an eye, foot, hand or deafness. The gold could be awarded for disablement or blindness.

The Wounded Badge in silver. The black and gold badges differed in frontal appearance in color only.

Infantry Assault Badge

Infantry Assault Badge in silver for infantry and mountain infantry. Motorized Infantry Assault Badges were awarded in bronze.

General Assault Badge

Tank Battle Badge

Tank Battle Badge in silver for tank crews.

Tank Battle Badge in bronze for "Panzer-Grenadier" and other armored fighting vehicle personnel.

Close Combat Clasp

The Close Combat Clasp was awarded in three grades: bronze, silver and gold for 15, 30 and 50 days, respectively, engaged in close combat.

Front and back – Close Combat Clasp in bronze.

Medal for the Winter Campaign in Russia 1941-1942. LEFT: Front and back as issued. RIGHT: Issue envelope.

The Italo-German Campaign Medal in Africa 1941

CHAPTER 7
DOCUMENTS AND PAPER ITEMS

This is the cover of a booklet designed to attract members of the Hitler Youth to the SS.

ABOVE: An SS newspaper of the times.

RIGHT and BELOW: An SS Police post card.

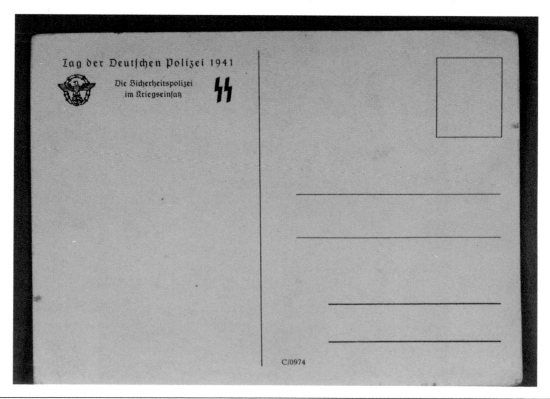

A period edition of "Mein Kampf " by Adolf Hitler.

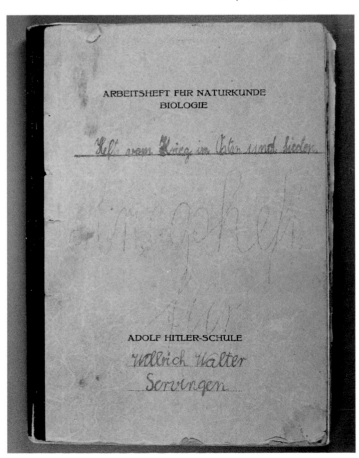

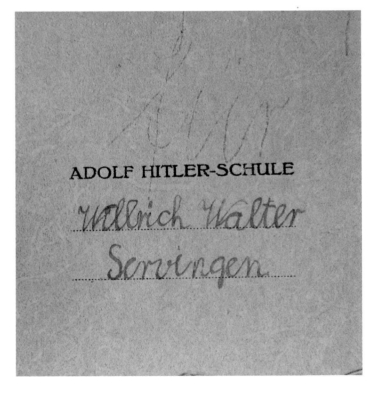

LEFT and ABOVE: A school-age child's biology workbook from Adolf Hitler School.

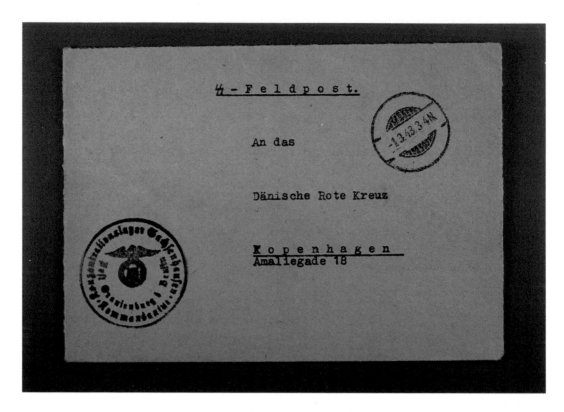

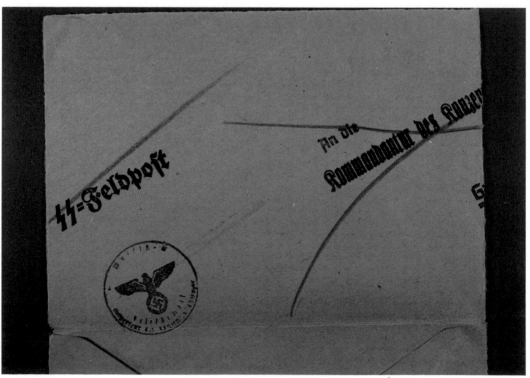

Covers of SS photo albums.

The ring beside it's issue box.

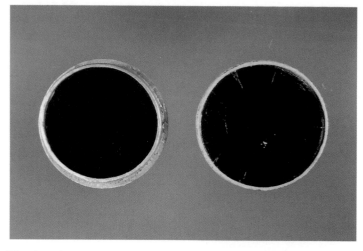

The interior of the issue box.

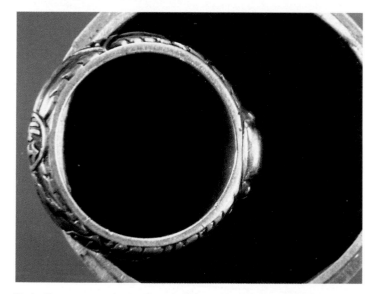

Note the seam where the skull is separately applied.

The date 21.12.43 is visible inside the ring.

"H. Himmler" signature engraving is visible inside the ring.

Recipient's name engraved inside.

The second example is well worn and was issued to Officer Hardieck on 20.4.40 (Hardieck's Allgemeine uniform is pictured in Chapter I).

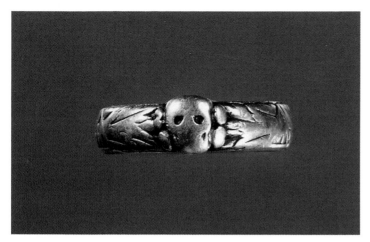

The well worn Honor Ring of Officer Hardieck.

Although heavily worn, it is still obvious that the skull is separately applied.

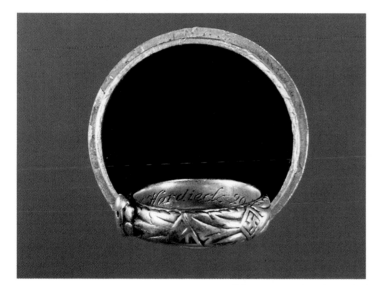

The engraving is still clear inside Hardieck's ring

Front and back – SS runes patch worn on the left breast by members of the SS Female Auxiliary.

SS Female Auxiliary signal operator's sleeve band.

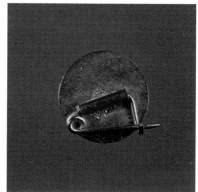

Front and back – SS pin.

LEFT and ABOVE: Front and back – SS belt in white leather for drummer. Note the drum hanger on the wearer's right front, below the waist belt.

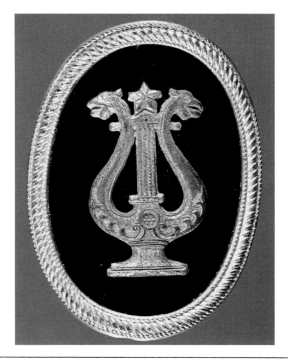

RIGHT: Front and back – SS Bandsmen sleeve band.

This violin is a well made instrument. It was handcrafted in 1941 in Dachau and features a hand carved SS eagle and runes in the peg head.

SS Runes and Eagle carved in peg head.

SS runes on reverse.

A portion of the "Dachau Musikfabrik" paper label is visible through the "F" hole.

The date 2.3.1941 is visible in this photograph. The paper label reads "Dachau Musikfabrik, 686,1732 SS, 2.3.1941, Rhane Greenberg # 19267."

A trumpet and banner of the Hitler Youth bearing the single rune.

The SS Standard Bearer's Gorget.

Front and rear.

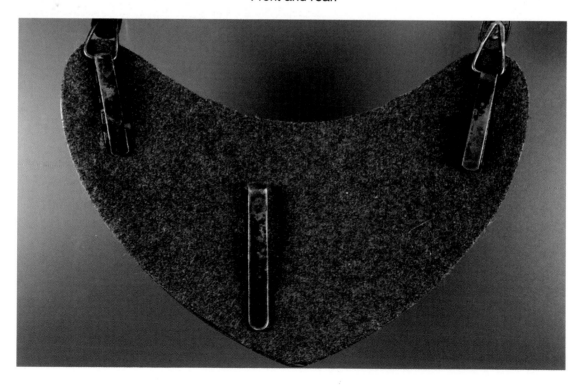

Detail of markings on one of the hooks on the back of Standard Bearer's Gorget.

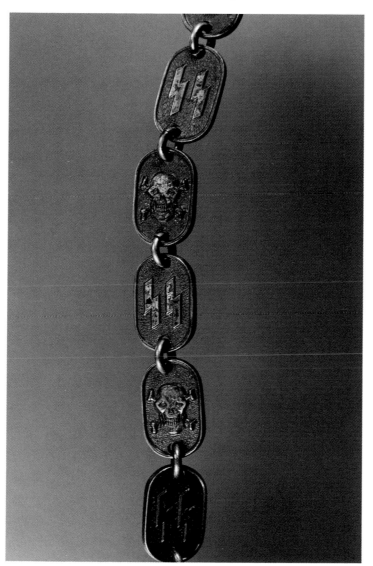

Detail of Standard Bearer's Gorget chain.

Note how chain is affixed to gorget hooks.

ABOVE and BELOW LEFT: Detail of the Bussing N.A.G. Medium Half-Track.

The Half-Track was equipped with an operating jack, which fit into the storage compartment. The electrical wiring visible in the compartment was for the operating headlights!

Detail of the K18 Field Gun.

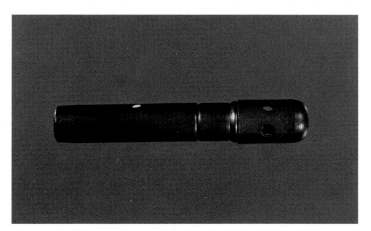

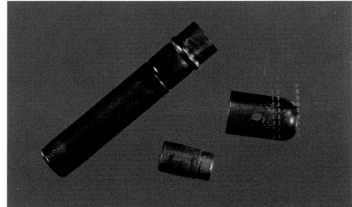

This container held the "shells" for the gun. Caps were placed in the shells and the gun could be "fired."

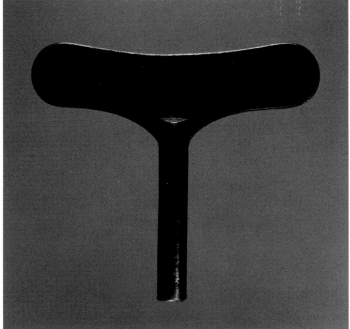

Caps, in the original box, for the gun shells.

This key was used to wind the Half-Track and it would move under it's own power!

This Searchlight Crew is another example of Hausser's quality toys.

The Motorcycle Troops

Details of the Motorcycle Troops.

Motorcycle Troops in action during the war.

Motorcycle Troops in action during the war.

CHAPTER 9: CHILDREN'S TOYS
The Allgemeine SS Figures

Original photo of Allgemeine Troops. Note the Sentry Box and its toy replica shown below.

Allgemeine SS Troops on parade.

Detail of the Goose Stepping Standard Bearer.   Detail of soldier.

The SS Band figures.

SS Troops in the traditional brown shirt uniform worn from 1932 to 1936.

An "Elastolin" Machine Gun Crew.

Musicians of the Hitler Youth.

An Allgemeine soldier "taking a break."

German soldier in great coat.

Hausser also made Elastolin figures of famous personalities of the Third Reich. A few examples are presented here.

Adolf Hitler

Ernst Rohm

Rudolf Hess

Paul von Hindenberg

Lineol was another maker of quality German toys. Here are several examples.

Staff car with Hitler figure.

A staff car similar to the Lineol example.

The Radio Armored Car with early Panzer Troop figures.

The Lineol Radio Command Car.

There is something ironical about this innocent looking doll in the sinister uniform of the Allgemeine SS!